The hard generative work of good preaching is to show the ways in which an old treasured text is as contemporary as the life we live today. I cannot remember when I have seen such a sustained embodiment of the good work of preaching. DeLoach has taken up both the plotline and the specificity of the Book of Exodus in order to summon us to fresh faith and to missional living. This is a series of sermons to which attention should be paid because Greg's word and our lives constitute a perfect match for each other. This book is an important gift we do well to receive and welcome.

Walter Brueggemann
Columbia Theological Seminary

Catching Up with God

Freeing Ourselves for Divine Engagement

C. Gregory DeLoach

© 2020
Published in the United States by Nurturing Faith Inc., Macon GA,
www.nurturingfaith.net.

Nurturing Faith is the book publishing arm of Good Faith Media (goodfaithmedia.org).

Library of Congress Cataloging-in-Publication Data is available.

ISBN: 978-1-63528-098-2

All rights reserved. Printed in the United States of America.

Scripture quotations are from New Revised Standard Version Bible, copyright © 1989 National Council of the Churches of Christ in the United States of America. Used by permission. All rights reserved worldwide.

Cover image by Anton_Petrus.

Acknowledgments

It is often said that gratitude is its own form of prayer, and I believe this to be true. Since no book or sermon worth reading is written without the markings of gratitude, this is as much a book of prayer as it is of sermons.

My prayer of gratitude begins with the many congregations who opened wide their doors and hearts, allowing me the privilege to stand behind pulpits and say a few meager words into their lives. I am especially grateful to the beautiful souls who gathered every Sunday at Unity Baptist Church near Summerville, Georgia. These good people took me in and claimed me as their pastor when I was a naïve but earnest young college student. Their generosity of love and gift of blessing has held me and kept me through the years.

Tiffany Stubbs, a student at McAfee School of Theology, worked over my manuscript, made suggestions, corrections, and encouragement. On her horizon churches will be as thankful as I am as Tiffany lives out her calling. Speaking of McAfee, Mercer University provides yet another context to live more fully into my vocation as I work with and learn from the students, faculty and staff.

I conclude with a prayer of gratitude for my beloved family. My father taught me to appreciate the gift of hard work and honest living, and he taught those lessons daily as a dairy farmer and daddy. My sons Clark and Aaron remind me how thankful I am that their lives completely changed my own life. Nothing I have or will ever accomplish will equal the gift they give to me by calling me daddy. Finally, my wife Amy does not always understand my wilderness wanderings in matters of life and faith, but has remained steadfast by my side all along the way. Her life is grace to me as we wander together.

Gratitude is prayer. Gratitude is life. Gratitude is really the only thing we can leave behind to share with others.

Ordinary time, 2020

The boundary lines have fallen for me in pleasant places;
I have a goodly heritage.

Psalm 16:6

Contents

Introduction 1

Missio Dei: Called of God   Exodus 1:1–4:31
  When God Is No Longer Believable   Exodus 1:1–22 4
  Getting Saved   Exodus 2:1–10 9
  Seeing Wrong   Exodus 2:11–15 13
  Does God See? Does God Hear? Does God Care?   Exodus 2:23–25 17
  This Call Is for You   Exodus 3:1–4:17 22
  Whose Side Are You On, God?   Exodus 4:18–31 27

Mission Dei: To a World Dislocated   Exodus 5:1–11:10
  Pharaoh Would Like You to Work Late   Exodus 5:1–6:1 32
  Name Dropping   Exodus 6:2–13 36
  It's a Hard-hearted World   Exodus 6:28–7:7 41
  Snake Handling Will Not Win You Friends   Exodus 7:8–13 45
  Frogs, Gnats, Flies—It's the Little Things   Exodus 7:14–11:10 50

Missio Dei: To a World Reimagined   Exodus 12:1–15:21
  When You Are Marked for Life   Exodus 12:1–28, 43–50 55
  The Costly Side of Salvation   Exodus, 12:29–42 60
  Don't Forget to Remember   Exodus 13:1–16 64
  A Failure of Imagination   Exodus 13:17–14:4 67
  The Other Side of Deliverance   Exodus 14:5–31 72
  "Who Is Like You, O LORD?"   Exodus 15:1–21 77

Missio Dei: A Wandering Journey   Exodus 15:22–18:27
  I'm Thirsty!   Exodus 15:22–27 82
  I'm Hungry!   Exodus 16:1–36 86
  Perhaps We Could Complain Louder?   Exodus 17:1–7 92
  Who Is Propping You Up?   Exodus 17:8–16 96
  You Cannot Do This On Your Own   Exodus 18:1–27 101

Missio Dei: A Covenant for Life Exodus 19:1–24:18
  Mountaintop Experience Exodus 19:1–25 106
  Ten Words to Live By Exodus 20:1–17 110
  Do You Read the Owner's Manual? Exodus 20:18–23:19 116
  Breaking Chains Exodus 23:20–33 121
  When Awesome Really Is the Only Word Exodus 24:1–18 126

Missio Dei: A Meeting Place Along the Way Exodus 25:1–31:18
  A Place to Belong on the Way Exodus 25:1–28:43 132
  A People to Belong with on the Way Exodus 29:1–31:11 137
  A Day to Belong on the Way Exodus 31:12–18 143

Missio Dei: In Failure and Restoration Exodus 32:1–34:35
  Lose Your Religion Exodus 32:1–35 150
  Facing Glory…and Surviving Exodus 33:1–23 155
  Learning to Get Along with God Exodus 34:1–28 159
  Face Up and Look Out Exodus 34:29–35 164

Missio Dei: A People at Work Exodus 35:1–40:38
  Saying Yes Exodus 35:1–39:43 170
  Finishing What You Start Exodus 40:1–33 173
  To God Be the Glory Exodus 40:34–38 177

Introduction

"In your steadfast love you led the people" (Ex 15:13).

I preached this collection of sermons while I served as the senior pastor of the First Baptist Church of Augusta, Georgia. We lived "thickly" for nearly a year in the ancient stories, following along with the narrative and theological arch of Exodus (the book that bears that title as well as the movement that defines the people).

The word "exodus" brings to mind urgent images of migration, flight, or escape. Rarely does one think of it as something generative and life giving. Exodus feels more like survival. Kurds in flight across Turkey, Iran, and Syria are described as being in exodus, with blood marking their steps. Children of El Salvador and Honduras are in exodus as they desperately pick their way through Mexico and into the United States. Hurricanes like Katrina push families out of their homes and neighborhoods and into migrations of transitions. Churches, too, are in their own kind of exodus, with the loss of privileged status, navigating through the wilderness of missional identity and theological wanderings.

Exodus is both an ancient story and a contemporary one. The book within the Torah called Exodus is the epic narrative of God's deliverance of the children of Israel that continues to speak to all who wander, seek, or flee. It is the story of a larger gospel of *Missio Dei*—the work or mission of God. The center, or subject and object, is with YHWH moving ahead, leading, calling, and summoning. Through Exodus we read of Israel's experience as part of the greater story of God at work in creation.

In the book of Exodus, we read of the LORD God working through the particular people called Israel to bring about liberation and deliverance and along the way we read of wanderings, apostasy, grumblings, and restoration. This is a story about a particular people in a particular time. And yet, it is also a story for all people groaning, murmuring, wandering, and searching for God to remember, direct, and work in their lives.

God is still at work in this world, from one generation to the next, in a mission of liberation and redemption. We are invited to join with God in that holy enterprise. In joining God, we also recognize our own need for liberation and redemption, as well as our call in and to a world of dislocation. Walter Brueggemann writes of the Exodus story, "…it provides for us the *essential characters* and the *recurring plot* that is always being performed and re-performed in the world."[1]

In Exodus, we witness a "contextualization" of the good news of God speaking to weakness and power, to enslavement and liberation, to deliverance and inheritance. As witnesses, we listen for our call of God, see the dislocation of our world, and re-imagine what could be. This work inevitably involves its own kind of wilderness wandering along with failures, sin, and broken faith. Yet YHWH invites us back into covenant and restoration as we move forward into a world broken and waiting.

The Latin term *missio dei*, the work of God, provides an interpretive framing of the sermons based on Exodus. Lesslie Newbigin and later Alan Roxburgh challenged the church to move from an ecclesiastically-centered mission to catching up to where God is already at work. As such, just as God was at work in the Exodus narrative and in the hearing and telling of it, God is also at work in our world today. The role of the community of faith is to discover how and where God is working and to join with God in that holy endeavor.

It is an old story and if we are honest in the telling, sharing, and hearing of it, we can at times find ourselves standing alongside the bloody Nile with Pharaoh, or trotting alongside it with some of the women. We may sympathize with the enslaved as we arise each day to make more bricks or as likely be discomforted and disturbed by our own complicity as the taskmasters disbursing burdens.

The old story is still a fresh story that people of faith and people wanting faith still tell because we still live in a world that needs to hear.

[1] Walter Brueggemann, *Truth Speaks to Power* (Louisville: Westminster John Knox, 2013), 16.

Missio Dei:
Called of God
Exodus 1:1–4:31

When God Is No Longer Believable

Exodus 1:1–22

God is at work in this world. I believe this as surely as I stand before congregations week after week. Not only is God at work in this world, God is at work in you and those around you. Since the Word was spoken and in the beginning of time the universe came to be, God has been at work. And I want to be where God is working. And I believe there is a deep hunger in others for the same. That is what we mean by *Missio Dei*—the mission of God, the work of God. God is at work, and to live purposefully is to be a part of where God is working.

We are a people on pilgrimage too, each with a personal journey as well as a congregational one. Exodus tells us about God at work in the people called a "treasured possession" (Ex 19:5). In hearing their particular story of God at work, we too can see a foreshadowing of our story that we are still speaking, telling, and living.

So let's turn to the story of Exodus and discover again how God was working and discover too how the *Missio Dei*—the mission of God—is still at work.

The story of Exodus begins with a bit of a history lesson because the writer knows that history is easy to forget. Some stay stuck in the past, that is true, but many of us just forget. When I was a young adult I took an active interest in researching my family history. This was before ancestor.com and Google, so I had to go about it the old-fashioned way—libraries, microfiche, and archives. I made some progress, but a funny thing happened along the way of researching my history—life. I was a young husband and was serving my first church as a full-time pastor. We had a two-year-old boy and another on the way. I no longer had time for history. Now that I am older and many of my kin are no longer around to tell the stories, I realize that I want to know more about my history, my people, and my stories, even the bad ones that others may want to forget.

And so the opening lines of Exodus connect us with a family history of ancient names like Jacob and his sons:

"These are the names of the sons of Israel who came to Egypt with Jacob, each with his household: Reuben, Simeon, Levi, and Judah, Issachar, Zebulun, and Benjamin, Dan and Naphtali, Gad and Asher. The total number of people born to Jacob was seventy. Joseph was already in Egypt" (Ex 1:1-5).

You remember Joseph, right? He was the boy with a coat of many colors and maybe a little bit of an attitude. Joseph was the one who moved from favorite son, to despised slave, to the second in command of Egypt—all in just a few short chapters in Genesis. Joseph was a hero to the old-timers of the past. Ah, but what a difference a few years and generations can make.

As quickly as we are given these names of ancient family history in the opening verses of Exodus, verse 8 practically leaps off the page: "Now a new king arose over Egypt, who did not know Joseph" (Ex 1:8). Did not know Joseph? Joseph, who helped save from famine not only his people but the all of Egypt? Because he did not know Joseph, it also means he did not know the God of Joseph who preserved Israel and Egypt. We are all just one generation away from a soul-less amnesia.

Who is this king in Egypt, anyway, whom the book of Exodus will eventually just call Pharaoh? According to historians, we can narrow down the possibilities to a few names: Sethos or Ramses II or Merneptah. What is interesting is that in the book of Exodus, Pharaoh is not given a name. Pharaoh is a title, not a name. Walter Brueggemann speculates that Pharaoh is never named, "Because if you have seen one pharaoh, you have seen them all. They all act the same way in their greed, uncaring, violent self-sufficiency."[1] By not naming Pharaoh, the book of Exodus reminds us that, in the end, Pharaoh will not matter, not count, and most of all, is not the point of this story of *Missio Dei*—God's mission.

It is enough for us to know that Pharaoh is the new king and, in spite of his vast holdings and imperial power, does not know some things. The fact of the matter is that not only does the king, the pharaoh, not know about Joseph and Joseph's God, let alone the people of God called Israel, it is clear that the king does not care. What the king cares about is not surprising: security, protecting ones' status, and empire building. These sons and daughters of Joseph had become numerous and Pharaoh saw them as threats—"They are taking over!" Pharaoh is more interested in his empire and protecting it than in the people whom God values. In verse 11, we read: "Therefore they set taskmasters over them to oppress them with forced labor. They built supply cities, Pithom and Rameses, for Pharaoh" (Ex 1:11).

In other words, Pharaoh had so many assets he had to build additional cities to house it all and forced the enslaved Israelites to do it. It reminds me of the story Jesus tells of the farmer whose crops came in and he had so much abundance that he built bigger barns. The story goes that the farmer turned out to be a fool because he would never live to see another day. All of his life was spent in accumulating and protecting while squandering the very life that was God's real gift.[2]

I could go on and on with other stories of Pharaoh, and we will hear more about him as we read Exodus, but you get the picture. Later in the chapter we read that he will resort to the murder of the Hebrew boys as a way to control the population. "When you act as midwives to the Hebrew women, and see them on the birth stool, if it is a boy, kill him…" (Ex 1:16a). Sound familiar? When Jesus was born, it was no silent night because Herod—the pharaoh of Jesus' time—ordered the same kind of slaughter. Every Hebrew boy in the small village of Bethlehem was killed and the infant Jesus escaped only because Joseph was warned in a dream.

We are tempted to make Pharaoh's fear and insecurity monstrous and therefore unbelievable, but we can understand. We have our own empires to protect, our own insecurities that run amok, and our own statuses to promote, even if it comes at the expense of others. That is when we better watch out because when we forget *who* we are we will also forget *whose* we are and the *Missio Dei* becomes just another Latin phrase.

"Now a new king arose over Egypt, who did not know…" That is the world Moses was born into. That is the world we are born into, too. We are born in fearful times and sometimes we are the victims of another's fears and sometimes, like Pharaoh, we can be the perpetrator. Pharaoh did not know who this Joseph was; let alone God.

Do you know? Not just your history and biblical heritage, but do you know who is God of the past and present, God who is still at work in our time? Do you know? It may not be so much a question of existence—that is, does God exist?—as it is a question of does God listen; does God care; does God matter? These are some of the implied questions not only in this first chapter of Exodus, but throughout Exodus. These questions are still being asked today. They are asked by the church, threatened with diminishing status in a culture that has moved beyond the church; they are asked by people who have left the church and by those who have never stepped foot in the church: Does God listen; does God care; does God matter?

These are questions of fear. Pharaoh was afraid, and so are we. We are gripped by fear and insecurity. Suddenly, children crossing the border become a threat because they are going to take our jobs in a job market that is no longer promising. Suddenly, we fear for the wellbeing of our own children—their choices and the consequences. Suddenly, we are worried that our little empire is not enough.

Those three questions about God—does God listen; does God care; does God matter?—are as ancient as Egypt and as current as today. The children of Israel throughout the book of Exodus will be challenged in each of these areas. Their answers will be varied but there will be times when some will say God does not listen; God does not care; and God does not matter. The very ones called a treasured possession will from time to time grumble, complain, threaten, and give up. We will read all about it.

What about for you? If God does not listen and God does not care, it is not so far to say that God will not matter. The king certainly did not think so. What mattered to the king was protecting his empire at all costs. Forced labor for the benefit of the few followed by a system that not only did not protect the people, it attempted to destroy them. When you believe that God does not listen, does not care, and does not matter, you are forced to live fearfully and reactively. Ironically, Pharaoh was becoming a slave to those he attempted to enslave, or as the Talmud teaches: "He who acquires a slave, acquires a master."[3]

This cycle of fear and abusive power is not just an "Old Testament thing." In John's Gospel, Jesus is brought before Pilate (or is it really Pilate before Jesus?). Pilate was an arm of Roman Imperial Power. At his words soldiers were mobilized. At his word lives were held in the balance. In that courtroom of sorts the epitome of Power met the incarnation of Truth. Pilate asks his questions of insecurity: Are you the King of the Jews? What have you done? And finally asks, "What is truth?" (Jn 18:33, 35, 38). When you are insecure, even with all the trappings of success and power, truth can be easily relativized.

The king called Pharaoh, and Herod, and the governor called Pilate, and all other guardians of power and economic security question what it is, exactly, we know and believe. "The king did not know..." and truthfully, there are times when we do not know, or forget, or just are not sure.

That is why we keep telling these old, old stories: because power keeps forgetting; because victims of power get tired of remembering; because all of us are prone to giving in to our lesser natures, our insecure selves, and like Pilate, we question the truth, and like the king of Egypt we just do not care anymore.

But God is at work. Pharaoh did not remember. Ultimately, what pharaoh forgot, or did not know in the first place, was that this story was not about him. It is about God at work and over and over again the stories in Exodus and throughout the Bible remind us that God is working in some unlikely places and through unlikely people. Later in this chapter of the book that never names Pharaoh, two Hebrew women are named—Shiphrah and Puah. They remembered what the unnamed Pharaoh did not know. They remembered and saved the lives of those Hebrew babies. The powerless enslaved women subverted the Egyptian king. They remembered that God listens and God cares and God matters.

When God calls you to be a part of the *Missio Dei*, God calls you by name. You can rest assured that your part in that call, no matter how insignificant it may look to you, can very well change the world. Just ask those like Shiphrah and Puah.

The *Missio Dei*—the mission of God—is God's story for God's people. Because God listens, God cares, God matters, and you matter to God. Don't you want to be where God is working, even if it puts you up against some pretty big names?

[1] Walter Brueggemann, *Truth Speaks to Power* (Louisville: Westminster John Knox, 2013), 17.
[2] Luke 12:13-21
[3] Kiddushin 20a

Getting Saved

Exodus 2:1–10

Ask anybody who has ever been in a delivery room and they will tell you that it is a miraculous place. When my boys were born, each event was as marvelous as if water had suddenly changed to wine, or a sea had been parted, and walking on water would not have been as impressive as those moments I shared in the delivery room. Sure, they looked like aliens all pink, wrinkled, and wet, but they were my aliens! You know how people say it is a miracle every time a child is born. I am here to testify it is true; it really is true. The delivery room can be a miracle room.

We have this story of a delivery room of sorts and it, too, was a miraculous place, but what is special about it has less to do with the event of Moses' birth—it only takes up about a half of a verse —as it does with the many other lives involved in his birth. The *Missio Dei*, the mission of God, is at work not because of how special Moses was in his grand infancy, but because of his mother, his sister, and the surprising introduction of the daughter of the Pharaoh. Unlike Shiphrah and Puah, the two Hebrew midwives who subversively acted against Pharaoh in the previous chapter, these women along the Nile are not named, but their deeds have been remembered through the centuries.

This is a story about God at work behind the scenes with rescue, deliverance, and ultimately salvation. The deliverance and salvation were not just for Moses, but for all the oppressed children of God. Power, no matter how dominating, impossibly oppressive, or complete is never free to disregard truth. In the shadows of Pharaoh's call for the destruction of every Hebrew baby boy, they stepped into the delivery room and, by doing so, participated in the call of God.

God is always at work. Sometimes we see, sometimes we do not, and sometimes we refuse to acknowledge the work of God even when it is right in front of us, like a baby in the delivery room, nestled in a basket. The *Missio Dei* is another way to speak of the Kingdom of God. Centuries after Moses, Jesus walked the earth and reminded us: "The kingdom of God is not coming with things that can be observed; nor will they say, 'Look, here it is!' or 'There it is!'

For, in fact, the kingdom of God is among you" (Lk 17:20–21). Elsewhere, Jesus says, "Let the little children come to me; do not stop them; for it is to such as these that the kingdom of God belongs" (Mk 10:14–15).

One day, along the River Nile, a basket floated along containing a little child and Egypt in all of its power never noticed that the very kingdom of God, the *Missio Dei*, was breaking out. It makes me wonder what God is up to today that is going unnoticed by all but a few. Why Moses? After more than 400 years of slavery, why Moses? What made him so special? To begin with, we know very little about his parents. They are not even named until the sixth chapter. Moses' father disappears after the first verse. Why does Exodus not name his parents until much later in the story? In a rabbinical commentary, an explanation is given, "To teach us that any Jewish family can give rise to a great person…as if to say: 'Perhaps this will be the one to make the world into the kingdom of God.'"[1]

I believe that Moses became of great use to God because in his earliest days three women unwittingly worked to give life, even when their culture pressed on taking life. The calling of God in the *Missio Dei* did not start with Moses the deliverer and liberator. It was already at work in the lives of three anonymous women. God is working today, right in our midst, whether or not we notice.

Based on the text this morning, we learn a couple of things about these women. First, they believed in life…not death. That may sound glib and much too obvious, but there are times when it is just much easier to believe in death, because death can be more believable than life. Robin Williams was, for me, as with many of you, a wonderful actor and comedian and I was shocked and sad when I read of his death, apparently of suicide. He suffered greatly and, in the end, could no longer believe in life, just death. I say this not unsympathetically, but by way of compassionate understanding. Life became too hard and death was all he came to know.

Death we see and believe in because it is all around us. We make death a statistic with Palestinians, Israelis, Iraqi Christians, and Kurdish Muslims dotting our headlines. We fear the death of Liberians languishing with Ebola, worried that it may be our death, too. And then, with our words we demonstrate our loyalty to death by making jokes at the expense of people we do not like or are afraid of and denigrate opposing political, religious, and denominational views. It is easier to believe in death. Therefore, we kill one another with our words, thoughts, actions, and inactions and in the end destroy ourselves.

When Moses was born, the Nile River stunk with death because that is what the Pharaoh believed in and he wanted everyone else to believe in it, too. But three women stood in the middle of the stench and said they will not participate. Even Moses' name is death defying. It has Egyptian origins, "Mosheh," but sounds like the Hebrew "masha," meaning, "to draw out." It calls to mind Psalm 18:16, "He reached down from on high, he took me; he drew me out of mighty waters."

The call of God is life affirming and, because it is God's work, it is what we are to be about, too. God invites us into this holy enterprise. Each woman played a part in giving, protecting, and providing life for Moses. There was of course his mother, who gave birth to him, and covertly kept him alive in spite of Pharaoh's death edict. There was his sister, who watched over the basket as it floated haphazardly down the Nile, and through her cunning skills had the baby returned to Moses' mother to be nursed. Then there was Pharaoh's daughter, who discovered the basket with the baby, took pity, and literally saved infant Moses from certain death. Even mighty Pharaoh could not control the life-bearing disobedience taking place in his own house. Contrast all of this with Pharaoh, who is markedly bent on death. He even distorts the Nile—seen as a place for life with its seasonal fertile floods—as a place for death. But the mothers in this drama step in and do exactly what is God's intention for this sacred work of *Missio Dei*—they believe in what God believes—life.

It begs the question: how are we living in life preserving, bearing, giving ways? Are our actions and responses contributing to death or life? While I read many heartfelt responses to the death of Robin Williams, I also read discouraging words that were judgmental and deadly. These come from those who believe more in death than they do life. Robin Williams reportedly said: "I used to think the worst thing in life is to end up all alone. It's not. The worst thing in life is to end up with people who make you feel all alone."[2] Remember, you could be life to someone who is drowning. Jesus said the kingdom of God is among you. Believe it.

One last thought regarding these life-affirming women of Moses. In these few verses we learn that they…acted with intention, which is another way to say they lived purposefully. Notice that in spite of a patriarchal society, where real power is male authorized and male centered, it is the women in this story who take charge. They did not wait for life to happen to them, although much was indeed happening to them. Rather, they each—in their own way—took initiative and lived in intentional ways.

Moses' biological mom knew the death-bearing politics of the day and acted shrewdly—a basket among the reeds. Moses' sister kept watch over the floating basket and brokered a deal with a princess. The daughter of Pharaoh discovered the basket, saw the baby, took pity, and even though she knew he was a Hebrew, defied orders and saved a life. In fact, we do not know if the Pharaoh's daughter ever had a child of her own. Was she infertile, barren? We do not know. All the Bible tells us is that she played a vital role in this baby's life.

You can have a purposeful role for God's mission by playing an instrumental role in someone's life. It wasn't like Pharaoh's daughter was looking to save a life that day. All she was doing was taking a bath—all in all, it was just a routine day. She did not even worship the same God as the Hebrews. She was just…there. Which is about all God needs of us…to be there.

The narrative is about the roles three women play because they believed in life and not death and in life they lived with intention and purpose. From this they unwittingly entered into the call of God for the mission of God. In this story, God is not named or even credited in this salvation narrative. God is silent. The hiddenness of God is made present in the lives of others. All because these women paid attention to life and did not simply resign themselves to letting life merely happen to them.

Jesus said that the kingdom of God is among you. At times it shows up like a laundry basket floating down the river. Each day we are graced with the opportunity to live, to dare to believe, and we are privileged from time to time to discover that the *Missio Dei*, the work of God, includes you and me. By doing so, we just may save someone's life.

[1] David L. Lieber. editor, *Etz Hayim: Torah and Commentary* (New York: Jewish Publication Society, 2001), 322.

[2] Robin Williams Quotes. BrainyQuote.com, BrainyMedia Inc, 2020. https://www.brainyquote.com/quotes/robin_williams_650958, accessed August 11, 2020.

Seeing Wrong

Exodus 2:11–15

I wonder if this story of Moses stepping in to avenge the beating of an enslaved person—a fellow Hebrew no less—is preached much in churches. Personally, I have never preached a sermon on this story and neither is it included in the lectionary. The inclination is to move from the marvelous and sensational birth story of Moses in the first part of Chapter 2 and leap over the rest of the chapter in order to get to the burning bush story of Chapter 3. Doing so makes the story of the call of God for the work of God just another simple, romantic tale without all of the messiness.

Life, however, is not usually that idealistic. It has bumps, bruises, and harsh realities that get in the way of poetry. Chapter 2 is where the formation of who Moses will *be* begins to take place. Have you ever said, "If God just spoke to me from a burning bush as with Moses, I would better understand God's will in my life"? Most of us, however, will never have a burning bush story. Notice that God did not start nudging Moses into a called life with a burning bush. It started much earlier, during just another ordinary day where what was wrong in the world finally was noticed.

I think the call of God for what we call the *Missio Dei*—the mission or work of God—occurred during this tumultuous, ragged time of God's silence in the midst of the world's chaos. While there are many places to begin the story, if we jump ahead to the burning bush we will miss an important part of the call of God. Do you ever find yourself somewhere "in between" chaos and clarity? It is precisely in these times between chaos and clarity that I believe we are being shaped and formed for a much greater purpose.

Starting with verse 11, we move from infant Moses drawn out of the Nile in a basket to a grown man. He walks about and sees the misery of "his people" in the shadow of Egypt's opulence, power, and empire, of which Moses has been a beneficiary. Where today we see pyramids and symbols of a successful culture as tourist attractions, Moses sees that something is wrong in the world, particularly his world—his adopted world and the world of his kinfolk. What you see (or don't see) in this world shapes how you hear the call of God in your life. To walk around blind and deaf to those around you is to also close yourself off to God's own voice calling and shaping you.

With verse 12, the response of Moses is initially problematic. He sees a fellow Hebrew being killed. In all the English translations I have read, it describes the scene as a beating or, as with the KJV, a "smiting." In the original Hebrew, however, it is the same word used with Moses' action against the Egyptian, which was to kill. The Egyptian is killing a Hebrew, so Moses the Hebrew kills the Egyptian. Is this about seeing wrong and responding? Which brings up another question: do two wrongs make it right? Moses hides the slave master in the sand knowing that at least legally he is in the wrong. The question of Moses' committing murder as justifiable is not answered.

When we get to verse 13, we read of another day, with more violence, except this is internal, between two Hebrew slaves. Once again, Moses steps in to stop the violence. Notice that he does not judge or reprimand. He stops the division and appeals to solidarity. "Why do you strike your fellow Hebrew?" (Ex 2:13). Moses does not yet know that the call of God will involve leading the people through even more conflict to get to a promise that will depend on the solidarity of the people. You cannot get to God's promise all on your own. You will need each other for the journey as well as for the sharing. Our pilgrimage with God is not a solitary journey.

In verse 14, we see that the intervention is not well received at all and Moses is now accused by his fellow Hebrew. Why? Was there resentment of Moses? Was the slave community now being punished for Moses' action the day before when he was standing up for the slaves? We do not know. The challenge to Moses' authority foreshadows what is to come when Moses answers the call of God to lead the people to the Promised Land. Israel will gripe, complain, and rebel all the way.

When you answer the call of God and enter into the work of God there are no assurances that you will receive the support you think you deserve. There came a pivotal point in Martin Luther King, Jr.'s work when the support of the Civil Rights community was dwindling. He was facing jail time in Birmingham and bail money was drying up. He was on the verge of irrelevancy. It was during this solitary time of isolation from within and without that he penned the now famous "Letter from the Birmingham Jail" that galvanized the Civil Rights Movement and has now been compared with the writings of Gandhi and Henry David Thoreau. Imagine where we would be if we never heard his words from "I Have a Dream," or "I Have Seen the

Promised Land." Gandhi, Dietrich Bonhoeffer, Nelson Mandela, to just name a few, failed to garner unequivocal support of the very ones they were trying to help. It goes with the territory.

By the time we come to the end of this story in the first part of verse 15, the words of the slave to Moses had the intended effect of threat and now Moses was no longer righteously indignant, but afraid. Pharaoh knows what Moses did and is out to do to him what Moses had done to the Egyptian. "When Pharaoh heard of it, he sought to kill Moses" (Ex 2:15). What is particularly tragic here is that Moses is rejected by Egypt, where he has held a home and presumably a place of privilege with the family of Pharaoh. It was Pharaoh's daughter who adopted and raised him, after all. Moses is also rejected, at least indirectly, by his own people. Somebody turned on Moses. He no longer has a home with Egypt or with the Hebrews. For a season that will span years, he is neither of Israel or Egypt and now must figure out who he really is because there is nothing left for him at home—wherever that used to be.

Have you ever been there? Where you were rejected and neglected and felt as though you had nowhere else to turn? Consider that it may be in that very place of wilderness-rejection where God is shaping and forming you for a greater work that cannot yet be imagined.

Moses flees and settles in Midian, which is an expanse of land that is nothing more than a desert, suitable for nomads, vagrants, and wanderers. He goes to the wilderness to find refuge and, we shall soon read, identity. Moses will find out who he really is. Who says Chapter 2 doesn't have poetry? The whole saga is both brutal and violent and seemingly tragic. Hebrew enslavement; Egyptian striking a slave; Moses killing the Egyptian; a slave striking out at Moses; Pharaoh seeking to do to Moses what Moses had done to the Egyptian; all under the shadows of the pyramid and the silent, watchful eye of God.

So what does all of this mean for us today where there are no pyramids in our backyards, but where we from time to time find ourselves right between chaos and clarity; the known and the unknown? First, it means that in between chaos and clarity, you too are being shaped for a part in the work of God, the *Missio Dei*. Epiphanies, voices from above, burning bushes, blinding lights, and signs along the way may come, but God's call begins first by paying attention and seeing and hearing and being willing to do something. When God is most silent, the real interior work begins.

Secondly, it means that though following the work of God into this world may be at times a lonely enterprise, it is a shared work that involves others. Individualism is a creation of modernity. Community is a gift of God rooted in creation. If you get to God's promise by yourself, you failed. While Moses flees to the wilderness because there was nothing left for him here, there will come a day when God will send him back to bring others along.

Thirdly, it means that there very well may be times in which, like Moses, you find your identity, your "self" challenged from within and without. It is in these periods of wilderness searching that you are given the gift to reassess your identity and connections and discover whom you really are.

Finally, it means that the call of God is often set where the world is most broken. And so we best pay attention to the streets of Ferguson, Missouri, and the villages of Liberia. We should see what is happening under the bridges where we live and sit awhile in the middle of broken families with broken hopes, many of whom come week after week to church. Where the world is most broken is where you will find the *Missio Dei* unfolding.

Jesus once preached a sermon based on Isaiah. Reading from the scroll handed to him, he said: "The Spirit of the Lord is upon me, because he has anointed me to bring good news to the poor. He has sent me to proclaim release to the captives and recovery of sight to the blind, to let the oppressed go free, to proclaim the year of the Lord's favor…Today this scripture has been fulfilled in your hearing" (Lk 4:18–19, 21).

Where in the world is God calling you? Who in the world does God want you to see? What in the world are you going to do about it?

Does God See? Does God Hear? Does God Care?

Exodus 2:23–25

When I was young, single, and in college, it seems I spent much of my time waiting for the pay phone just down the hall from my dorm room to ring. I know I was in school to study and discover new truths, but I was dating Amy and books no longer had priority over my schedule. I did not want to call her collect and I never seemed to have enough quarters to pay for my call, so I waited to hear from her. She was the one, you know. The one I had been waiting for all of my life. Oh, the waiting for love and that phone to ring! Silence can be deafening, especially when you are anxiously waiting to hear from someone: a call, an email, a text—anything to provide a bit of hope or assurance that all is well and all will be well. If you have been on the receiving end of a pathology report, you know all too well what it feels like to wait in silence while your misery commandeers your imagination. We have been there with God, too: waiting for a word, a nod, or at least a glance to reassure our fears and our anxieties.

This is Israel in our text today. Though God has been mentioned a few times in the first two chapters of Exodus, God has been passive and silent. Meanwhile, we read of kingly insecurities that lead to murderous conclusions. A baby of no particular merit is saved from this tirade of infanticide because three women step in. This child grows up and makes some mistakes and flees the scene in exile and fear. Meanwhile, God is quiet.

Four words from the Hebrew vocabulary speak volumes in this context of silence: "groaned," "cried out," "cry for help," "moaning" (Ex 2:23–24). It is not a pretty scene. Even though the personified object of their oppression, the pharaoh, is now dead, we are told their suffering is alive and well and so far, God is missing. It was hoped, since the old pharaoh died, that the new king would follow the tradition of granting amnesty and relief from the Israelites' plight but their hope in the new regime, whatever it was, was misplaced. Their cries move from the empire, to themselves, and finally to God.

It sounds a lot like Job, another character from our Bible who is remembered as the embodiment of suffering the indignity of God's silence and apparent absence.

We need to stop right there and linger for a moment or two around the phrase "absence of God." It sounds disloyal to say it, let alone think it. It has an air of apostasy to it. Yet, it is a valid expression in the Hebrew tradition. Listen to this Psalm to get an idea of a cry of absence:

"How long, O LORD? Will you forget me forever?
How long will you hide your face from me?
How long must I bear pain in my soul,
and have sorrow in my heart all day long?
How long shall my enemy be exalted over me?" (Ps 13:1–2).

And this is certainly not an "Old Testament thing." We remember dark Gethsemane and the anguished prayer of Jesus asking to have the cup removed. There was also his disturbing cry from the cross that exclaimed God's forsakenness.

Have any of those words ever spoken for you? Now I realize that most of us enjoy the peace and prosperity of western civilization and have a comparatively privileged lifestyle compared to much of the world. We typically do not hear this text in the same way as oppressed people. It begs of us to ponder, who are the voices of those in the world today who cry out from their suffering, injustice, oppression? They fill our prisons and visit our food banks. They blanket our screens with images of sickness, hunger, and war. They are the Christians suffering in Iraq; the Buddhists beaten down in Burma; the Jews and the Palestinians dodging mortar fire and suicide bombers. They are the poor in Appalachia and in Atlanta.

We do not have to be oppressed, however, to know what it means to "cry out." Sometimes the only faith left is the crying and groaning in words that cannot be uttered. They are the broken prayers of broken people. Paul voices this in Romans 8:26, "And in the same way the Spirit also helps our weakness; for we do not know how to pray as we should, but the Spirit Himself intercedes for us with groanings too deep for words."

This is not a text primarily concerned with guilt. Rather, the agenda is the capacity to be honest enough about the pain—the pain of others and the pain we carry about us. "Pain publicly processed turns to energy."[1] We should know that from the cross. Hope is the confession that things do not have to stay the way they are.

Remember the story of a blind man named Bartimaeus in the Gospel of Mark? He knew all too well his pain and his suffering, and in the story he would not be silenced. When Jesus was leaving Jericho, Bartimaeus cried out for Jesus' mercy. The crowd tried to silence him but suffering cannot, in the end, be silenced and Bartimaeus wanted mercy not pity. Stories like this in the scripture remind us that a theology that passively and politely waits on God and simply leaves it to God is not the only way to God. Israel groaned, cries out, and moans...and God hears... "Their cry for help rose up to God. And God heard..." (Ex 2:23b–24a).

Why now? Why does God respond now? We will explore how and in what way God responds in later chapters in Exodus, but for now it is enough to ask why; why does God respond now? Is it out of pity? Compassion? Perhaps, but more fundamentally, the response of God is rooted in memory.

"And God remembered his covenant..." (Ex 2:24). God made a commitment to Israel long ago and God still believes in Israel. It goes back to Genesis 12 when God calls Abraham out to be a unique people of the earth. "I will make of you a great nation, and I will bless you, and make your name great, so that you will be a blessing...and in you all the families of the earth shall be blessed" (Gen. 12:2–3). Notice that this is not about Abraham as privileged or special, but about the responsibility of being a blessing to the world. This is a way, if you will, for God to shine throughout the world. It is in part what we mean by the *Missio Dei*, the mission of God.

God remembers this covenant made with Abraham some four hundred years later as Israel languishes in slavery and misery in the heat of the Egyptian sun. God remembers and still wants the children of Abraham to be that blessing to the world, to allow the light of God to shine to the nations. In a Rabbinical commentary on the Torah, a writer quotes Abraham Heschel defining Jewish religion as "the awareness of God's interest."[2]

Of course, to say that God remembered is somewhat problematic as it is with the other verbs of hearing and seeing and noticing. It could imply that God forgot and now the misery of Israel has jogged the divine memory. More likely, it is that in the fullness of time, events, people, and places, now the time has come where God moves from silence into response.

What is interesting to read is that this story is "time-stamped." The king of Egypt dies and a new king replaced him, but this new king will not make any difference. Hope will not come in political progress. The difference we find out will come through the people of Israel saying "enough"—their cries for help "rose up." In the fullness of time the people say there must be something more. Leaders will emerge, miracles will unfold, and the voice of God will thunder out. But now, at this moment, something is stirring within the people.

It is the voice of Sojourner Truth leading both blacks and women into emancipated freedom. It is the stirring of Desmund Tutu speaking against apartheid. Has there ever been a time for you when you found yourself saying, "enough!" Are you willing to believe that surely God has something more in store than present circumstances allow?

God works in the fullness of time and events. This is not just about God getting around to doing something. This is about God inviting you to be a part of the great cosmic work that began in creation and will end in the new creation. As one writer phrases it, "God's waiting for the right configuration of human and natural events to put a new level of activity together with respect to this situation."³

This is not just about God finally getting around to doing something. This is about God doing something through others. In this passage, we see that the time is right for Israel to shine again in redemptive ways. Yes, we know, God will send plagues, part the sea, feed the masses with manna from heaven, and be visibly present in pillars of cloud and fire. All the while, God will also be working through the very ones who are to be liberated and set free.

Could that still be true? I very much believe it so. First, because God wants the blessing to go out to all the world. This still includes Israel, but through Jesus we believe it is also through you and me. Secondly, I believe this to still be true because the world is still as messy as it was thousands of years ago. And just as it was of old, God's response is shaped according to the fullness of time, events, and people. We have seen this to be true through the ages. Two thousand years ago, Israel found itself in occupied territory and their oppressors were Romans instead of Egyptians. Prophets were silent but a young peasant girl heard a voice from heaven and she said yes. A baby was born in Bethlehem and Rome was too arrogant to see that their world was about to change.

What part will you play in being the blessing, the miracle, the voice of healing and freedom in others? Here is the thing: it still comes back to God initiating. Hear the words of our text as the blessing and commissioning it will become: God hears, God remembers, God sees, and God takes notice. Let us not neglect what catches the attention of God, because that is where God is working—the *Missio Dei*. And where God is working is where I want to be, too.

[1] Notes from a lecture by Walter Brueggemann, September 21, 1992.
[2] David L. Lieber editor, *Etz Hayim: Torah and Commentary* (New York: Jewish Publication Society, 2001), 32.
[3] Terrence E. Fretheim, *Interpretation: Exodus*, (Louisville: John Knox Press, 1991), 47.

This Call Is for You

Exodus 3:1–4:17

This is a message about God calling us to live a purposed life and this particular story of Moses' call will guide us. This reminds me of an old, old joke. A thief broke into a house one night. As he was shining his flashlight around, looking for valuables, he heard a strange, disembodied voice from the dark saying, "Jesus is watching you." He nearly jumped out of his skin, clicked his flashlight off, and froze. When he heard nothing more, after a few more moments he shook his head, promised himself a vacation after the next big score, then clicked the light back on and began searching for more valuables. Just as he pulled the stereo out so he could disconnect the wires, clear as a bell he heard, "Jesus is watching you." Freaked out, he shined his light around frantically, almost dropping it in horror. Looking for the source of the voice, his flashlight beam came to rest on a parrot perched off in the corner. "Did you say that?" he snapped at the parrot. "Yep," the parrot confessed, and then squawked, "I am just trying to warn you." The burglar relaxed. "Warn me huh? Who are you?" "Moses," replied the bird.

"Moses?" the burglar laughed. "What kind of stupid people would name a parrot Moses?" The bird promptly answered, "Probably the same kind of people who would name a Rottweiler Jesus!"

Usually the call of God is not as direct as a Rottweiler, nor as invasive. But sometimes God's call does come in strange and unusual ways. This could be said of Moses. I know that burning bushes or voices from heaven are not the norm for most of us, but anytime we feel a nudge, or the stirring of a still, small voice, or find confirmation of a purpose, we find ourselves on holy ground. The very act of removing shoes in the custom and culture of the Middle East was a sign of hospitality and being welcomed home. Imagine God inviting Moses to remove his shoes as a way of welcoming Moses home, as if God were saying, "You have finally found what you have been looking for."

Let's look at Moses' holy ground moment. Moses, it needs to be pointed out, is currently dwelling on the west side of the wilderness. He grew up privileged, but ran afoul with the authorities and now spends his time tending sheep. They weren't ever his sheep. They belonged to his father-in-law. Shepherding, especially for your father-in-law, was no golden parachute for this man formerly of Pharaoh's house, but this is how it is when you are living on the west side of the wilderness. That is where you go when you are on the run, escaping the disappointments of your past.

Some of you know what it feels like because you live on the west side of the wilderness, too. You are working a job that makes you feel miserable. You have children who are not making good choices. You did not get accepted into a particular college or you just did not get the chance to go to college. Let me make a sweeping statement, but I believe it to be accurate: sooner or later we will all spend some time living on the west side of the wilderness where life has taken a disappointing turn.

For Moses, God is calling him out of the wilderness of disappointment and into a purposed life. And to think, Moses is eighty years old at this point in the story. One would think that the time for purpose is in the rearview mirror! Just a typical day—at least that is what Moses thought. But this would be the day when holy and mundane intersect and Moses would never be the same again. You have all heard the story since your childhood. A bush is on fire, but it is not burning up. Moses thinks to himself, "I am seeing things." Then if that is not strange enough, the bush is talking. Well, there is a voice coming from the bush. "Great," Moses probably is thinking to himself, "Now I am hearing things." He is, after all, getting on up there in years.

This strange and unusual encounter with God was not simply for Moses' own enrichment. It was a call for purpose that would be much larger than the security of the family business. Indeed, much larger than Moses' own imagination that anything would be different. God tells him, "I have come down to deliver…and I will send you to bring my people out of Egypt" (Ex 3:8,10).

Sure, I know what you are thinking: "This is about Moses, but I am just… me." Please remember that the *Missio Dei*—the mission of God—is a calling that has been at work since creation to bring about hope, healing, deliverance, and salvation to a lost and broken world. God is inviting us all to be part of this holy work. A call of purpose is a call to live for others. The holy ground is where we get that nudge, that affirmation, that call that God is very much interested in moving us from the west side of the wilderness of predictability and security to the places of purpose that contribute to a better world.

This is not about a job or a career. My friend Dock Hollingsworth, who is the pastor of Second-Ponce de Leon Baptist Church has written, "God does not appear to Joseph and tell him to be a carpenter or the Apostle Paul and tell him to be a tent maker. These are jobs—they are not purpose. Some people find purpose in their work but all people can find purpose in their part in God's redemption project. All people can help the suffering and afflicted and be part of what God is doing in the world."[1] What God is doing in the world is what we mean by the *Missio Dei*.

I know that we all have our list of excuses of why our life does not have a purpose or why the timing is not right or why this is for someone else. Moses had excuses too—five of them, to be exact.

Excuse #1—"Who, me?"

Moses asked, "Who am I?" (Ex 3:11). "You have the wrong guy, God. Your celestial database has crashed." We know that kind of question, that kind of excuse. In the face of awesome challenges and in the vacuum of leadership, we sneak to the back of the room and say, "Who am I?" Most of us feel like we don't have the authority, the wisdom, the street-smarts, the relevance, the political savvy, the backing or support of others, or any other litany of excuses to respond to God's call to lead a purposeful life.

But in verse 12, we hear God's response: "I will be with you." In fact, more than twenty times in the Old Testament, God assures those whom he has called that God will be with them.

It is the assurance of presence. It doesn't matter who you are—Moses, Mary, Joseph or Greg or Debbie or Bill or Elaine. God is going to be with you, be with us. Existential anxiety gives way to holy presence.

Excuse #2—"Who are you?"

Moses asked, "What is [Your] name? What shall I say…?" (Ex 3:13). God's response: "I AM WHO I AM." It is from this verb that we have the name Yahweh. We really do not know that is how it is pronounced, but assume that the name sounds something like that. It is from the verb to be. Oh yes, it is an enigmatic response. Yahweh's disclosure is a reminder of sorts of the Lord's power and sovereignty and sufficiency. I am who I am and that is good enough.

Biblical scholars will tell you that the name, in the end, essentially means, "I will be God for you." It is more of a reminder that what you know historically about God can be translated into personal experience. Everything we know about the God of history is reliable today. God is creator. God is source of life. God is powerful. God is able. It is not just history. It is reality. To the question, "Who are you?" God reminds, "You know who I am. I am who I am."

Excuse #3—"But suppose they do not believe me?"

Moses is saying, "They will not trust me. They will not listen to me." God has already assured Moses of his presence, and that history can be reliable when envisioning a new future. But it is not good enough. Moses is anxious, not just for himself and his own insecurities, but about what others are going to think.

And of course we have heard it all before. We value the perception of others. But not just about the consumerist opinions of others. We are anxious that maybe our faith may put us on the outside of public opinion. God's response: "What is that in your hand?" (Ex 4:2). It is a staff of course; a tool of a shepherd. It is used for support. It is used for defense. It is used as a tool to nudge and protect. Forgive me for oversimplifying the text here. I may even be guilty of dumbing it down a bit. Simply put, Yahweh, through a series of wonders, demonstrates to Moses that you have everything you need for God to use you against the doubt and disbelief, even your own doubt and disbelief. These are anxious times, which translate into anxious faith. Your speech, your talents, your career, your family, your looks, your smarts—you have everything you need for God's good purposes.

Excuse #4—"I don't talk pretty."

Well, literally, Moses uses the excuse, "I have never been eloquent…I am slow of speech" (Ex 4:10). Easily, we could slip in our own litany of excuses based on talent. Not just eloquence—although that's a good one. One quarter of the population lists public speaking as their number one phobia. But there are other excuses—see if any of these ring a bell: "I am not educated enough… I am not wealthy enough…I am not attractive enough…I don't have the right degree…I have too much to lose…I am not old enough…I am not young enough."

God responds: "Who gives speech?" (Ex 4:11). Moses forgot his Sunday school lessons. Yahweh reminds Moses of basic theology. God creates. God sustains. God has a purpose. When Moses speaks, it will be God speaking. God doesn't need the most qualified, or the perfect or the pretty. Noah was a drunkard; Sarah was an old lady; Ruth was an immigrant widow; Saul was emotionally unstable; David was hot-tempered; Solomon was a womanizer; Mary was a young peasant girl; Peter was uneducated; Matthew was a swindler; Paul was a persecutor; and Jesus was born homeless and raised by a man who wasn't even his father, who was a nobody from a forgettable village.

Excuse #5—"What about Plan B?"

Moses pleads: "O my Lord, please send someone else..." (Ex 4:13). God can use you to accomplish a bigger purpose, but you can refuse God. Theologians call this free will. If we refuse, God moves on to other options. The mission of God will not change just because of our excuses, but we will miss out on a purposed life. Instead of making life, we will just make a living.

What is standing in your way? What excuses are you using that have domesticated the power and relationship that God wants to have with you for your life and for this world? Spoiler alert: God got through to Moses and we read: "So Moses took his wife and his sons, put them on a donkey and went back to the land of Egypt; and Moses carried the staff of God in his hand" (Ex 4:20). The staff that at once was the symbol of Moses' disappointment was redeemed to an instrument of God's salvation. God had already given Moses everything he needed for what awaited his "one wild and precious life."[2]

What's your excuse for not allowing God to be God for you; for not allowing God—in the strange and unusual or the mundane and predictable—to dream something wonderful in your life? A professor in a class I was taking some years back remarked: "I am the only me that will ever be. Lord, what are you dreaming in me?"

What do you think God is dreaming up for you? Will you respond? How will you respond? When will you respond?

[1] Dock Hollingsworth, sermon dated January 12, 2014.
[2] Mary Oliver, *House of Light* (Boston: Beacon Press, 1992), 60.

Whose Side Are You On, God?

Exodus 4:18–31

The previous message was based on the familiar story of Moses and the burning bush. The voice of God calling and commissioning Moses after so many years—so many decades—and now, finally, Moses is heading back home with a sense of mission and purpose. His life will matter.

This next story is concerned with, "what happens now," and so it begins with a homecoming of sorts. The former "Prince of Egypt" is coming home. Moses left Egypt as a young man of passion and with a sense of righteous indignation. But he also left because he was outside the law. He is coming home as an old man now who has *not* made a name for himself. In fact, he may not even be remembered by anybody beyond his family. Even the old Pharaoh is dead. It is like coming back to visit your old high school only to realize that not only are all your former teachers gone, but no one remembers you and no one even cares.

Nevertheless, he comes home with a sense of purpose; a mission authorized by God. He no longer holds the shepherd's staff as a symbol of failure. It is now, as we read in verse 20, the "staff of God" and will be an instrument of God's salvation. We are told that God will use Moses for "wonders." Who doesn't want to be of use by God that way? To know that your life is purposed by God and God will use you for wonders is heady stuff. When I was ordained a few decades ago, serving my first pastorate, I thought the title "Reverend" would open doors for me, and that folks would respect me and value my opinion, and that I would now possess knowledge and insight that would relieve the suffering around me. I still believe in my calling and purpose and that it is of divine origin, but I no longer hold on to the illusion that to be called of God means that others will care or respect or value how God is using me.

Moses will find this out, too. In fact, in that same verse where God tells Moses, "See that you perform before Pharaoh all the wonders that I have put in your power," God goes on to say that Moses will not be met with instant success. "I will harden his heart…" (Ex 4:21). Pharaoh will have a hard heart. In Exodus, we read 20 times about this hard heart of Pharaoh. The biblical understanding is that basic psychological functions, behavior, morals, as well as spiritual life are concentrated in the heart.

Half the references sound like Pharaoh is hardening his heart and half the time it sounds like it is an act of God. Did God cause Pharaoh to have a hard heart, or did Pharaoh already have a hard heart and so it predetermined the actions to follow? I cannot satisfactorily answer it, but I do know that when my heart gets hard, it also gives me a hard head where I no longer listen to the opinions, ideas, and suggestions of others. My grandmother called it stubborn.

We see this played out on a national scale. Political theorists suggest that there has never been a time in our nation's history where we have been so divided along partisan lines. Republican and Democrats are finding it impossible to believe that the other side has any good ideas for our country. As a nation, which includes our own backyard, the data is pointing that we are more polarized than ever—confrontational, suspicious, fearful, and insecure. We rarely listen to opposing views, let alone respect others while recognizing real differences.

In biblical terms, it is called a hard heart. Pharaoh had one. I am less inclined to think that God gave it to Pharaoh, as I believe that God used Pharaoh's hard heart against him. Pharaoh's heart became his destiny. Look at what hardened Pharaoh's heart: In verse 22, we are introduced to a sweeping claim God is about to make of this enslaved, impoverished, and powerless people: "Israel is my firstborn…" Moses is to tell Pharaoh you have mistreated a child.

Think about how serious that claim is. As a pastor, you probably see me as an overall gentle guy. I laugh a lot, I am playful with others and I would not be described as quick-tempered or hard hearted, let alone violent. But if you mistreat my child, nothing will stand in the way of me making it right. This should give all of us who are in positions of power and influence a moment to reflect that throughout the scriptures God sides with those who have no voice, who have no advocate, who are powerless to help themselves. In Psalm 41:1, we read: "…How blessed is [the one] who considers the helpless; the LORD will deliver them in a day of trouble." All of us are to be attentive to those who are mistreated. Through Moses, God is serving notice, "You have mistreated my child." It is quite an audacious thing for YHWH, for God to say, in so many words, "you have mistreated my child, Israel; now I am going to mistreat your child." Is this a metaphor or a foreshadowing of the death and destruction that is to come because of Pharaoh's hard heart? Do you know anyone who is so stubborn that they will actually bring harm upon themselves and others just because they do not want to change their heart?

This chapter ends with an affirmation that God is paying attention to those most in need of attention and the response of Israel is nearly stunning: "The people believed; and when they heard that the LORD had given heed to the Israelites and that he had seen their misery, they bowed down and worshiped" (Ex 4:31).

While God did not get through to Pharaoh because of Pharaoh's hard heart, God does get through to Israel because of their hurting heart. Time and again, we are reminded that it is difficult for God to get through to those who assume they are doing just fine on their own. There is a story in the Gospel of Matthew where Jesus calls Matthew to be one of the twelve disciples. Remember now that Matthew was a tax collector and we can presume that he was despised by the religious community as a traitor and a cheat. That night there is a dinner party where other tax collectors and sinners show up and Jesus is criticized because he is surrounded by miserable company. To this Jesus says, "Those who are well have no need of a physician, but those who are sick.. 'I desire mercy, not sacrifice.' For I have come to call not the righteous but sinners" (Mt 9:12–13)

The people called Israel knew they were sick; their hearts were broken, and Moses wanted them to know that God has heard and wants to do something about it. Did you notice their response? "…they bowed down and worshiped" (Ex 4:31). For those of us who see worship as a service to attend, this may be confusing: Will it hold my attention? Is it novel? Will I be inspired; entertained? Authentic worship comes, at least in part, when we realize God doesn't need our hard hearts, just a ready heart; a listening heart; a contrite heart. Doing our very best is not what will give our life meaning and purpose. God is not calling us to "be all you can be" in worship or in the rest of life. God is calling on us to be part of God's own work of paying attention that we may be part of healing, deliverance, and salvation. And when we find what we have spent our life looking for in God, we are drawn to bow down and worship, because it is truly holy ground.

To recap:
1. Moses came home with a renewed sense of mission, where his story finally fits into God's story.
2. That purpose did not mean instant success.

3. The hard heart of Pharaoh not only got in the way of Moses, it got in the way of Pharaoh experiencing God.
4. God does not side with oppressive power and exploitation, but claims Israel as a firstborn child.
5. When Israel realized God sees, God cares, and God wants to do something through others, worship was the response.
6. As such, we are being invited into God's great work going on in the world from the very beginning of creation; even today—*The Missio Dei.*

"The people believed; and when they heard that the LORD had given heed to the

Israelites and that he had seen their misery, they bowed down and worshiped" (Ex 4:31).

Are you ready to finally come home and discover how your story fits into God's story? This will not mean instant success, at least how the world defines success. Is a hard heart getting in the way of you experiencing the living God of mission and purpose? When you see what God sees—the broken lives of others or your own brokenness—does it move you to worship and begin anew? Moses wasn't the only one standing on holy ground last week. We just might be right now.

Mission Dei:
To a World Dislocated
Exodus 5:1–11:10

Pharaoh Would Like You to Work Late

Exodus 5:1–6:1

Moses is joined by Aaron and together they are living into God's mission to the world through the treasured people of Israel. What an exciting place to be: in God's will; answering God's call; participating in God's work. I strongly believe this is God's hope for you and me and all of humankind. You and I are not random acts, destined to live out according to the whims and events of others. *The Missio Dei*—the mission of God—is to discover, at long last, after all this time, that you have finally found how your story fits into God's story.

So off Moses and big brother Aaron go with barely a pause and find Pharaoh and give him the words burning in their hearts. We have heard them before in song and poetry and drama: "Let my people go." We usually stop there. We think that they are calling for the emancipation of the enslaved Israelites. "Set them free, let them pack up and find a new place and a new home. Let them go or else." But that is not what they say to Pharaoh. Look again: "Thus says the LORD, the God of Israel, 'Let my people go, so that they may celebrate a festival to me in the wilderness'" (Ex 5:1).

I find it interesting that the first intended act of God is not to liberate the Israelites from Pharaoh. It is to first liberate them from themselves by stepping away for a time from what has occupied all their time. They are asking for a few days off. They are not asking for better wages, more vacation, or better insurance options. They are not asking to change the production quotas. Moses and Aaron are simply asking for a time for Israel to step back, rest, and worship and renew. They need a reminder that they are valued by God and that they value God. They belong to God and God belongs to them.

Do you take time to remember whom you belong to? In marriage, one pledges to belong to another. On a higher plane, worship and prayer and renewal are acts to remind us who we all, ultimately, belong to: "…your body is a temple of the Holy Spirit within you, which you have from God, and that you are not your own…" (1 Cor 6:19).

Pharaoh would like you to think differently. He wants you to work late because Pharaoh needs more bricks. He scoffs at Moses, denies any knowledge of God, and says: "Moses and Aaron, why are you taking the people away from their work? Get to your labors!" (Ex 5:4). And then Pharaoh ups the quota and wants them to do more with less. They will have to gather their own straw for the bricks. In the previous flowchart, the taskmasters provided the straw, which acted like a binding agent for the bricks. You had to have straw to make strong bricks. Now they not only must make bricks, they have to spend additional time gathering straw. Do more with less.

We may think and state that life is not about making more bricks, yet that is precisely how most of us spend our waking hours: more, more, more. More money; more time; more things; more production; more education; more promotion; more retirement; more life insurance—more, more, more. The very real problem of making more and more bricks is that there will never, ever be enough bricks for all the pyramids we are building.

Have you ever worked for Pharaoh?

I worked for Pharaoh once. No, I am not talking about my dad or any former church I served, although parents and churches can certainly be taskmasters! When I was a college student, I worked one summer for a transportation company loading transfer-trailer trucks for delivery. Packages by the thousands would come off of a conveyor belt and I sorted them by zip code and loaded them on the appropriate trailers. The supervisors had a system of calculating how fast and how accurately you loaded the boxes per hour. I could never get ahead and the packages kept coming. As fast as I loaded one truck and it pulled out there was another one waiting to back into the dock to be loaded with more parcels for delivery. I found out just why this was called the graveyard shift.

Have you ever worked for Pharaoh and realized that not only will you never get ahead, it will never be enough? Furthermore, you are just another brick maker, another cog in the machine, a minor player for a major corporation. Pharaoh values productivity. God values personhood. When God commands that the people leave their brick making for a time of worship, rest, and renewal, it is a holy reminder that the people are worth more than anybody's bricks.

Are you Pharaoh?

Here, I am not just talking about where you are on the company flow chart. Personally speaking, I can be unyielding about what I expect of others to the point of being unreasonable. People just don't always measure up and while high expectations are good, there can come a point where there is just no grace. Are you one of those demanding more bricks from others, even though life is really not about bigger pyramids? Are you one of those who expect so much from everyone else that you find you have exhausted meaningful relationships? When people become things to you to be exploited or used for your own gain, you just might be a Pharaoh.

Pharaoh values productivity. God values personhood. If you are Pharaoh, you best stop measuring your pyramid against others and value what God values.

Have you become Pharaoh to yourself?

Perhaps the worst taskmaster in my life is the one in the mirror. Notice one of the things Pharaoh said to Moses in verse two: "Who is the LORD…I do not know the LORD…" (Ex 5:2). Pharaoh did not know the God of Israel because he thought *he* was the god of Israel. Pharaoh thought himself to be a god. All those pyramids we read about in Egypt were the homes for each of Pharaoh's notions of divine immortality. Pharaoh thought himself a god. The troubling thing is that we too often believe more in Pharaoh than God. That is why we make more bricks instead of resting in faith and trusting in the worship of Creator God.

Several years back, I read a book I was supposed to read in high school or at the very least college, but instead waited until I was around 40. Moby Dick may very well be one of the greatest novels in the English language, so it is to my regret I waited so long to read this classic. In one scene, Captain Ahab and his small crew are on the whaleboat madly rowing out to the great white whale *Moby Dick*. Men are flaying and sweating against the oars trying to outrace the elusive whale. All are pressed into this singular task except for one man: the harpooner. He does nothing but sit idly and quietly by while all the others do the work. Melville then has this great line: "To insure the greatest efficiency in the dart, the harpooners of this world must start to their feet out of idleness, and not out of toil."[1]

That line from Melville reminds me of the beloved Psalm, "Be still, and know that I am God" (Ps 46:10), or Isaiah's "In returning and rest you shall be saved; in quietness and in trust shall be your strength" (Isaiah 30:15).

No calling, no mission, no work can be carried out, in God's name, apart from stepping aside, re-centering, and remembering through worship and

Sabbath that the LORD is God. Recall what I said earlier in this sermon: the first intended act of God is not to liberate the Israelites from Pharaoh. It is to first liberate Israel from themselves by stepping away for a time from what has occupied all their time.

When you are re-centered and reconnected with YHWH God and not some imposter called Pharaoh, you find that your value is not centered on how many bricks you can make. Your value is in personhood, not productivity. The deliverance that is to come is not simply from their labors. It is deliverance into a new identity. "I will take you as my people, and I will be your God" (Ex 6:7).

The sweep of the story of Exodus, indeed the entire Bible is this: God takes us from bondage, to release, to inheritance. We have Noah and the flood, Abraham, Sarah and the promise, Jeremiah and the exile, just to name a few examples in the Old Testament. Of course, the ultimate embodiment of God delivering from bondage, to release, to inheritance is in the cross of Jesus with the deliverance from sin and the promise of eternal life. Every time we baptize, we are telling the story again—bondage, to release, to inheritance. And every Sunday we gather, we are here to remind each other that God is still in the redemption business.

But we will not believe any of this if we believe more in Pharaoh than God and just stick to our bricks. What is it that you have not yet given over to God? God wants to deliver you and redefine you. It is time to rest, worship, and renew. "Let my people go" are the words of God to Pharaoh. It is time to let go and let God claim you and name you.

[1] Herman Melville, *Moby Dick* (London: Penguin Classics, 2002), 274.

Name Dropping

Exodus 6:2–13

Our biblical journey through Exodus took a slight turn in the last chapter. The movement is from a call of God to looking at the world God has called Moses to serve—and that world was a mess. Pharaoh's world, the Egyptian's world, Israel's world, and now our world is dislocated, that is, it is not where God intended. It is a mess.

Today the headlines tell us about Ebola virus and the plight of West Africans. Over in the Middle East, ISIS is threatening Christians, Muslims, Kurds and taunting our own sense of security here at home. Speaking of home, in our own land we are buried with slogans and hashtags that bespeak brokenness: #metoo, #blacklivesmatter, #prochoice, and #prolife are just a few of the many indicators of our national dislocation. Not only are countries broken but so is the earth itself. According to a recent press release, the world is pumping more and carbon pollution into the air as the earth continues to warm and political leaders debate causation. The world was and still is not where God intended. Tell me, what are you planning on doing about it?

In this dislocated world of Moses, Aaron, Israel, and Egypt, listen to what God has to say:

> "I am the LORD
> I will free you
> …and deliver you
> I will redeem you
> I will take you as my people
> I will be your God
> I will bring you…
> I will give it to you
> I am the LORD" (Ex 6:6–8).

All of these assurances are given and can be depended upon because God said it. God tells Moses to do some name dropping. "I am the LORD." We read that claim no less than five times in this one chapter. Earlier in this passage, God reminds Moses: "I appeared to Abraham, Isaac, and Jacob as

God Almighty…" (Ex 6:3). Many of us have learned along the way that the name "God Almighty" is *El Shaddai* in the Hebrew. That is a name that describes God. God is mighty, *El Shaddai*. To the great patriarchs, God was known by description, but not personally. Verse three makes clear, "but by my name 'The LORD' I did not make myself known to them" (Ex 6:3). YHWH is the personal name, the intimate name, and so Moses gets to know God not just descriptively but personally.

Name dropping. Have you ever done that? Often on Facebook I read of friends and church members who drop names of important people. A recent glance at my Facebook page revealed one friend who had lunch with Justice Clarence Thomas, and included a picture. Another friend posted a picture with Hershel Walker, both smiling broadly for the camera.

Moses is told to name drop and tell Israel that God has these promises and so you can count on it—and not just any generic God either. Go on Moses, you can name drop. Tell them:

"I am the LORD
I will free you
…and deliver you
I will redeem you
I will take you as my people
I will be your God
I will bring you…
I will give it to you
I am the LORD" (Ex 6:6–8).

Those are solid assurances, no matter who you are. Three things are said by YHWH: 1) I am present, 2) I am faithful, and 3) I will set you free. Yet in spite of these assurances, verse nine is revealing at this point in the drama: "Moses told this to the Israelites; but they would not listen to Moses" (Ex 6:9). In time, we will get to know Israel better and we will read of how they do not listen because of their fear and fickleness. We will hear stories of their own hard hearts and complaining and murmuring and open hostility that get in the way of listening, but not at this point in the story. We read that they did not listen, not because of stubbornness but, "because of their broken spirit and their cruel slavery" (Ex 6:9). The original Hebrew that many translations have as "broken spirit" literally reads "shortness of breath."

I sympathize. It is hard for me to hear God's word of hope and deliverance when all around me the world, especially my world, is broken. "They would not listen…because of their broken spirit." You probably know what that is like, too. You cannot get a job and your prospects look meager and some well-meaning soul says, "Well, God's got a plan." I am sorry, but that kind of talk is not very helpful. Maybe there is some truth in it, but is that what you really want or need to hear?

You sit on the cold examining table and hear the words "cancer" and never hear another word that day, and some friend says, "God's will be done."

You find yourself beneath a tent covering the grave of someone you loved more than your own life and you feel a hand on your shoulder and someone whispers, "We will all be together one day."

These may very well be promises of God, but when your spirit is broken, you are too bound up to hear them. "They would not listen…because of their broken spirit and their cruel slavery."

Who can listen when your spirit is broken and your misery is so great? When you have been disappointed one time too many, your spirit is broken. When you have lived more in the house of despair than the house of hope, your spirit is broken. When you know pain as your daily friend, your spirit is broken. When the color of your skin or gender or sexuality leads to judgment and marginalization, your spirit is broken.

This is Israel. They cannot hear the words of hope, not because they are stubborn or hard-hearted, but because all they know is that they have been a slave to misery. "They would not listen…because of their broken spirit and their cruel slavery."

What is interesting here is that God's message (and disclosure) does not make it to Pharaoh because the people cannot believe anymore and their despair has permeated Moses: "The Israelites have not listened to me; how then shall Pharaoh listen to me, poor speaker that I am?" (Ex 6:12). Moses, we have heard these excuses before and God has given you assurances, even bringing in your brother Aaron to partner with you.

Are you seeing the pattern here? Everyone, including God, has a communication problem. God is speaking, but nobody is listening. Israel cannot hear because they are too broken. Moses is not listening because he still does not believe God can use him. Everybody has a communication problem—YHWH, Moses, and Israel. And it is all because of despair from bondage.

What is it in your life, today, that has you bound and despairing and has so robbed you of imagination that you cannot fathom that even God can do anything about it? Go ahead; name your slavery. Are you the mother worn out and tired and while you are pouring your life into your family you are not sure who *you* are anymore? Are you the one who can barely keep your head above water, living from paycheck to paycheck, tossing during the night wondering how you are going to pay that next utility bill? Is your slavery your career, going nowhere; your health, falling apart; your stress, eating you from the inside out?

Go ahead, name it, name what has you captive. Chances are when you identify the misery of your own bondage, you will be better positioned to hear anew what God has to say.

Even when we don't hear or cannot hear because of our brokenness and because we are too enslaved to our excess or neglect, it does not change what God has to say in this dislocated world and our dislocated lives. "I am YHWH, your God…I am present…I am faithful…I will set you free."

In our worst or darkest of places; when we have been broken just one time too many; when the very world itself collapses around us, God's presence, fidelity, and mission of freedom will not be thwarted—whether we listen or not.

Israel will be set free and make it to the land promised to them. That is going to happen.

Yet the world will continue to break the spirits of others, so God kept speaking anew the same promises of deliverance and freedom. God spoke through kings and judges, through prophets and pilgrims, through big names and no-names. In time, God spoke to a peasant couple who named their baby "saves" or "sets free." This child grew up and walked into villages and cities proclaiming that God so loves the world. He was so serious about it that he allowed himself to be the very "broken spirit" for the world and died for it.

But the "Broken Spirit" did not stay broken, did he? The resurrection is the church's proclamation that even when you cannot hear through your own broken spirit, God has a truer word and lasting word than your brokenness. "I am YHWH," which means in part, "I am to set you free."

So when we hear the name Jesus, we hear the same name that means freedom: freedom from brokenness; freedom from all that has held you down or back; freedom from all that is working against you.

> "I am the LORD
> I will free you
> …and deliver you
> I will redeem you
> I will take you as my people
> I will be your God" (Ex 6:6–7a).

This is God's message to Israel, even though at the time they could not hear it. Still, it did not stand in the way of what God was setting out to do. It is, I firmly believe, God's message to each of us, too. And even if we cannot hear it, it will be done. It is God's message to this world. While we cannot make others hear, we can join in the living, working, and in the proclamation of God's deliverance.

It's a Hard-hearted World

Exodus 6:28–7:7

The theme within the larger drama of Exodus is the *Missio Dei*—the work of God—to a world dislocated. The world is not where God intended it to be. The old-fashioned word for this is "lost." Nowadays it is hard to get literally lost. GPS satellites can pinpoint with great accuracy where you are located, so, technically, you are never lost.

Yet the world is still dislocated and lost. We are not where God intends us to be and you and I are invited to work in this world. In Matthew 18:14 we read, "So it is not the will of your Father in heaven that one of these little ones should be lost." If this is God's will that not one little one be lost, then it ought to be our mission, too.

To guide us in this dislocated world, we have this rather droll passage of God, YHWH, doing most of the talking. I suppose my first reaction to this particular text is that it is, well, boring. There is not much action at all going on. In time, we will read about plagues, the Red Sea parting, and the Ten Commandments written by the finger of God. But right now, it is just plain dull.

The last half of Chapter 6 is a family history—a second one in Exodus—which generally not very interesting if it is not your family. In fact, it is not even a family history. It is the division of the tribes of Israel. Thrilling, right? And what about the first part of Chapter 7? It does not add any drama, mainly because it is a recap of previous statements:

1. I am YHWH…tell Pharaoh. We have already heard this seven times so far in Exodus.
2. Moses' excuse, "I am a poor speaker, why would Pharaoh listen to me?" This is the third time we have heard this one.
3. YHWH tries to bolster the old boy up, one more time, and tells him to speak what YHWH commands. Over and over again we have read and will read of this.
4. Oh, and by the way, God will harden Pharaoh's heart, or depending on the verbs, Pharaoh will harden his own heart. Previously, I noted about

Pharaoh's hard heart—a recurring theme throughout this episode. This is not the last we will hear of it.

This is becoming the groundhog day of biblical stories: a call to a broken world filled with broken people, but weariness and doubt in the call, and there are hardened and disbelieving hearts all around. It is a biblical treadmill of redundancy. And we have heard it all before.

If you and I are not careful, we might get bored in church. Have you ever gotten bored in church? Talk about asking the obvious! I think as long as there has been a church, there has been boredom. It is biblical. Remember the story about Eutychus in Acts Chapter 20? Paul was preaching a sermon, the place was warmed by lamps burning, and Eutychus goes into a deep sleep and falls out of the window. If that is not bad enough, Paul revives him and then continues to preach until daybreak!

Growing up, I did not get bored much in church worship. It wasn't that the worship during my childhood was that exciting. We had no choir or praise band or orchestra. I rarely recall special music to break up the monotony and the preacher was some old guy that smoked cigars in the parking lot. It was a country church, but I was rarely bored. This is because my daddy played the piano: three hymns and an offertory, after which he would sit down with all of us on the front pew of a church that would hold about 50 people. Two of us on one side, and two of us on the other and my daddy would drape his arms over our shoulders. On his right hand he wore his college ring from Auburn University, and I promise this ring could look you in the eye during those church services. Who can get bored with the threat of a thump on the head that could stir you to attention!

But back to our story here in Exodus: it is a biblical treadmill of redundancy. And we have heard it all before. Maybe that is the point. Sure, fireworks in the form of plagues and stunning supernatural acts will happen, but at this part of the story it is the same old call, same old world, same old enemies, same old assurances, and the same old stubbornness and disbelief.

The hard heart of Pharaoh stops up the ears of a fresh call, a renewed sense of purpose, and the imagination to see things differently. Recall that while we are told about Pharaoh's hard heart, Moses seems to have a doubting heart. God wants to use Moses but Moses cannot believe God on this one. Moses cannot imagine anything different for his life. How is your heart doing today? Hard? Doubting? Indifferent? Fearful?

Sometimes we get bored in church, not because we are not suitably entertained, but because we either stop listening or cannot imagine God calling for us to do anything different than the treadmill we are on. We may even excuse it as, "Well, I am just not getting fed."

Meanwhile God is trying to get through to Pharaoh's hard heart and Moses' fearful heart. Pharaoh refuses to hear; Moses cannot believe what he hears; and we are growing restless with this repetitive saga. Maybe God can do all of this without us, but for some reason God does not leave it alone. What is amazing is how God keeps at it. Walter Brueggemann puts it succinctly, "God's resolve awaits human readiness."[1]

God is working to bring about deliverance and freedom, healing and salvation, help and hope, but amazingly, God wants to work through others in this holy enterprise. Since creation when Adam was asked to tend the garden, we have been invited to partner with God. Jesus demonstrated this in one of the most memorable miracles—the multiplication of fishes and loaves. It is a story that is found in all four Gospels. The multitudes follow Jesus and the disciples and they are hungry for hope, for direction, for meaning and purpose. And they are also hungry for food. Now we know how this story ends. He takes five loaves and two fish and feeds the thousands sitting along the Sea of Galilee. The synoptic Gospels tell us before this miracle of God's deliverance, Jesus says to the disciples, "You give them something to eat." The disciples thought Jesus' words were nonsense.

The disciples are not that much different than Moses, who on three occasions tells God, "I am a man of faltering lips…I am poor speaker…I have [literally] uncircumcised lips." God's resolve awaits human readiness.

Yet God, one more time, invites Moses into this work that will not only change Moses, and give Moses purpose, but change a people and change the world.

One more time, God reminds Moses that YHWH is God.

One more time, God reminds Moses that he will not be alone.

One more time, God reminds Moses that Pharaoh will be hard hearted and not listen.

One more time, God reminds Moses he will lay his hand on Egypt and the Israelites and deliver the people into freedom.

One more time, God tells all of this to Moses.

Pharaoh and Egypt have stood in the way of God's work of life and blessing and God is not going to overlook it. Pharaoh's hard heart is not going to get in the way and neither is Moses' fearful heart. By the way, there is a very real and implicit warning to all who stand in the way of God's work for life while people and systems threaten it.

God stays at it with Pharaoh, with Moses and Aaron, and of course with us. Our own hard hearts and bored lives and the routines that slip into redundancy may rebuff God, but only for a while. God calls, God nudges, God reminds, God works, God sends, and God stays at it.

Remember Peter in the New Testament? He is the guy who steps out of the boat and falls through the water. He is the one who confesses Christ but denies the sacrifice. He is the one who warms himself by the fire when Jesus is being accused and denies him three times. He is the one who runs away in the dark weeping because of his failure yet again to be faithful. And he is the one who, for some inexplicable reason, God keeps coming back to and is used to start the first church in Acts and through his preaching three thousand were added to the movement of God.

God is doing a mighty work in this world and we are invited into that partnership, but some of us are not listening. Like Pharaoh, we have grown stubborn and hard hearted. Or like Moses, we are fearful and doubt we are of any use because we are not skilled or too old or too young. Some of us are not listening but that will not stand in the way of God.

And then we read, in a very undramatic, even dull way, "Moses and Aaron did so, they did just as the LORD commanded them" (Ex 7:6). With perhaps a bit of irony, we are reminded that they were 80 and 83 respectively. Not the age we associate with taking on a new calling in life. Who says older folks can't change?!

God is not going to give up on you, young lady. God is not going to give up on you, old man. God is not going to give up whoever you are because this lost world is too important for God to let a hard heart, or a fearful mind, or bored life stand in the way. The world is not where it is supposed to be. Are you?

[1] Walter Brueggemann, *New Interpreters Bible Commentary* (Nashville: Abingdon Press, 1994), 737.

Snake Handling Will Not Win You Friends

Exodus 7:8–13

Several years ago when I was travelling in New Delhi, I saw some amazing things just strolling along the sidewalk. I remember a vender selling food to be sacrificed at one of the Hindu temples. Not far from the vendor, a fellow sitting on a crate was stenciling tattoos for customers. Sitting, walking, limping, and languishing, I saw faces of human misery begging for coins and food.

Did I mention the monkeys? Monkeys were everywhere because the temple nearby venerated monkeys, so it was a particularly safe place to hang out. At one corner of the sidewalk there was a man playing a flute with a crowd around him. I thought he was just a street musician like you see in our country. When I walked closer to hear better, I also could see better. He was not a musician, but a snake charmer! How does snake charming work anyway? There I was, live and in person, watching this strange and frightening trick.

This story in our Bible begins with a snake and a magic trick. We have read of the calling, of the encouraging, of the sending, and of the empowering to go and participate in God's work of liberation. Go to Pharaoh, the king of Egypt, the captor of the Israelites, and perhaps the most powerful man on earth and…do a magic trick. In verse nine, we read that Pharaoh is going to ask, "Perform a wonder." This is not Pharaoh asking to be entertained. He is saying, validate that you really are called of God.

When I was a little boy, like many little boys, I was fascinated with magicians. I read a biography on Houdini, who was sort of a magician, and I marveled at the mystery that surrounded this complicated man. I think I may have even bought a few little tricks here and there along the way to becoming whoever I was becoming, but I was a fairly lousy magician. My sleight of hand was not so sleight and often I would forget "the trick" of the trick. Even if you do not like magicians, you cannot help but appreciate a good trick. "How did he do *that*?!"

God tells Moses and Aaron to go to Pharaoh and do a trick. Moses, I guess, was a lot like me and was not sure he was up for the performance, so

Aaron gets the job. We read the Aaron takes his staff, throws it down, and it becomes a snake. Few things will get your attention better than a snake appearing out of thin air. Snakes for the most part do not bother me, but a snake, nevertheless, will get my attention. A snake certainly got the attention of Pharaoh—albeit briefly. Pharaoh matched Aaron's act by bringing out his own magic troupe and they apparently know a magic secret. By the way, it is interesting to note the dynamics. Neither Moses nor Pharaoh is the "magician," they are "heads of state" and have others to do their bidding. Moses may not be good at magic, but in God's work he is superior to the more credentialed Pharaoh.

Pharaoh's magicians throw their staffs down and they too become snakes. But Aaron has one more trick up his sleeve. His snake eats up their snakes. How would you like to go to that show in Las Vegas? The word for snake is literally translated as sea monster or dragon. In fact, in all the other passages in the Bible where this Hebrew word is used, it is either sea monster or dragon. It is also the same word given to Pharaoh in Ezekiel 29:3, "I am going to deal with you, O Pharaoh, king of Egypt, mighty monster."

Is the point of this story about who is the better magician? Hardly. We need to adjust our terms as we seek understanding and application. What is happening here is a contrast between miracles and magic. Magic involves imposing our will on others. Notice that the magicians of Pharaoh utter incantations and spells as part of the act. They are, as any good magician will do, manipulating the environment and the audience in order to perform a good trick. The purpose is to impress and fool another by manipulation of reality.

Aaron is not acting as a magician because he does nothing other than throw his staff down. His purpose is not to impress or fool or otherwise trick Pharaoh or anybody else. Aaron is a vessel of God's mission to the freedom-bearing work at hand: deliverance and salvation. *Magic* involves imposing our will on others. A *miracle* is different. A miracle is the power of God beyond our categories. Pharaoh thinks that by sheer force or manipulation or magic he has the upper hand to a bunch of slaves and their stuttering leader. What Pharaoh fails to grasp is that magic is no match for the miracle of the deliverance by God.

There is a reason why we call the birth of a child, for example, a miracle. We certainly participate in this child's life, but ultimately we cannot give it life. That belongs to God. We can plant a seed in the garden, but we cannot make a seed and we cannot make it grow. That belongs to God. We can mimic all kinds of acts of nature but in the end we cannot produce anything. We can distort, we can manipulate, we can even bring changes, but we cannot make out of thin air anything. It all comes back to the Creator.

Miracles are part of a larger design, a greater gift that only God can give. Let me simplify this story by breaking it down into basic parts:

1. The power of God is a force for liberation. This is not about sticks being changed to snakes. It is about God's vision to set the people free from what has them bound.
2. There are others working against God through manipulation, trickery, and enslavement. All of which attempts to stand in the way of God's vision.
3. Ultimately, God's work and God's mission will swallow up all enemies of God's impending saving work of deliverance.
4. Still, like Pharaoh, many will refuse to see, believe, and participate in what God is doing in this world seeking to bring freedom.

Here is what I want us to be thinking about in light of this text: what are the sticks we are throwing down to the ground, magically believing that they will give us the same thing that God is offering? What are the substitutes competing against the freedom-bearing will of God?

You see, God not only wants to set the Israelites free from their captors, God wants to set you free, too. Name your walking sticks.

1. Money and the belief that more things will buy you satisfaction.
2. Power and the illusion that it will bring you peace.
3. Success and the hope that it will give you fulfillment.
4. Security and the assurance that everything is going to be all right.

Or maybe it is just good old-fashioned fear. Fear is, for many of us, the snake that we are handling or trying to charm because we are afraid.

Think with me about the many voices of magic out there making the claim that they can transform your life and make it better, capitalizing on our fears. "Buy this car and you get the sex symbol that goes with it…Buy this gel and your hair will be thicker and you will look younger…take this pill and all your problems will go away…choose this career and you will have status…drink this beer and you will be the most interesting man in the world. Wall Street, Madison Avenue, Hollywood, Washington DC, and all the other magicians want you to believe their bag of tricks, but you will still be enslaved, not much different than those ancient Israelites.

In the end, it is all an illusion, a sleight of hand, and a parlor trick that is doomed to be swallowed up. They may look real, feel real, and behave real, but they will not last. The magicians of Pharaoh and the magicians of our time will say that their staffs are just as good—and they are partly right. That is they will look real and feel real and seem real for whatever it is we think we need. All of it, however, leads to death.

Only God has what is real for this world and those held captive to Pharaoh and his troupe of magicians and it will swallow up the rest. Paul has this great line that I believe has many layers of meaning: "Death has been swallowed up in victory" (1 Cor 15:54). Death, after all, is the great snake that we spend all of our lives trying to charm.

What is false in your life that needs to be swallowed up by God, so that you can be set free to be the person God created you to be?

I thought about that very question recently with a group of pastors and together we discussed our personal struggles with the need for approval. While there is nothing wrong with the love language of affirmation, personally, I often treat it as an incantation for validation; the magic of applause. What I need is for God to swallow this up because my faith teaches me and my reason guides me and scripture affirms to me that God wants to set me free from all of this magical thinking. Through Christ, I am loved and set free.

There is this story in the Gospel of John when many followers of Jesus started leaving. His church, you could say, was declining. What Jesus was saying was difficult and following him was a challenge. As people were drifting away, he asked the twelve disciples: "Do you also wish to go away?" Peter spoke for the rest and said, "Lord, to whom can we go? You have the words of eternal life" (Jn 6:67–68). I want to experience the Holy Power of God that will set me free and swallow up all this other stuff. As Paul puts it, "Even though our outer nature is wasting away, our inner nature is being renewed day by day" (2 Cor 4:16).

The *Missio Dei*, the mission or work of God, is to set the people free from their bondage, their illusions, their false gods, and all the other lookalikes. It is time to stop snake handling and thinking you can charm these fakes. God has a powerful word; a liberating work; a vision to set the people free and will swallow up all the other charlatans that stand in the way.

So, if in the end, God wins, freedom will happen, then you and I get this chance to participate in this Holy project. This God, YHWH, wants to take us in and set us finally and forever free. Don't let a hardened heart get in the way. It will not stand a chance. Pharaoh, we shall see, will learn this.

Frogs, Gnats, Flies— It's the Little Things

Exodus 7:14–11:10

Last Sunday, I brought in a collection of walking sticks because the scripture was about changing staffs into snakes. Today the text is about frogs, gnats, flies, and other plagues on Egypt. From walking sticks transformed into snakes, we find ourselves reading about a few other divinely appointed nuisances.

Allow me to summarize the next five chapters: Eight times Moses will tell Pharaoh to "Let my people go." And each time, we will read of a plague—there will be ten of them, which in Hebrew numerology is a number for completion. This is going to get ugly, as in completely ugly! The plagues increase in destruction. It would take too long to comment in detail on each of the plagues. Here is a simple summary:

Plague #1 The Nile Turns into Blood—The very symbol of life for Egypt, the Nile, is transformed as death. Its waters affect the waters throughout Egypt. Like red tides experienced along the Gulf Coast, the stench of death and infertility is everywhere.

Plague #2 Frogs in Your Pillows—the scene is nightmarish: frogs in your pots, pans, and pantry; frogs in your bedding and your clothing. Frogs everywhere. When they died at Moses' command, we read in 8:14 that the land stunk. With the last plague, we are told that the river stank (Ex 7:21). The Egyptians are literally saying, "Things stink around here."

Plague #3 Gnats (or *Lice*) from the Dust—Basically, the plagues have affected the waters, the land, and now the air. No one, even folks from South Georgia, want to put up with gnats. Furthermore, the dust that became gnats calls to mind that from dust you are created and to dust you will return. Death is in the water; death is on the land; and now death is in the air.

Plague #4 Swarms of Flies—Maybe not a direct threat, but swarms of flies are more than a nuisance. Nature is rearing its head and crippling the empire. Besides, with death in the water, on the land, and in the air, flies are bound to follow.

Plague #5 The Death of Livestock—Livestock is currency. You trade it, you farm it, and you eat it. Livestock are no good dead.

Plague #6 Boils—Ever had a boil or some other infection on the skin? This is the first plague that is a direct physical assault. Now boils are a pandemic problem of misery for Egypt.

Plague #7 Hail—Today we typically only worry about hail because it can ding our cars. For agrarian societies, hail destroys not just livelihood, but food. The threat is hunger for today, and starvation for tomorrow.

Plague #8 Locusts—Hail is bad enough for a crop, but at least some of the remaining produce will survive. Locusts eat everything that is left. The devastation is near complete.

Plague #9 Darkness—This may not seem so bad to us, but when there is darkness where there should be light we know something is not right. It is a reversal of the Creation story where God separated the light from darkness. Think of it as a return to chaos.

Plague #10 The Death of the Firstborn—I suppose this one does not need any explaining. The firstborn was the investment for the next generation.

Some have attempted to explain the plagues scientifically. Each plague can be explained away—from the bloody Nile to the death of the firstborn—through natural phenomena. I read an article years ago interpreting the plagues as a lesson from environmental destruction. This is what happens, in other words, when you mess with "Mother Nature."

Like the rest of these stories, the intended lens of interpretation is theological. What is God about in this latest installment of Exodus? The plagues give a stark picture that everything Pharaoh has trusted in, believed in, and greedily kept and protected for himself has been dismantled and destroyed. In fact, the plagues attacked the many gods venerated in Egypt— the Nile was revered as the crocodile god *Sobek* of fertility; frogs were associated with the goddess *Hepat*, who assisted in childbirth; flies with the god Beelzebub, the protector of their land; and the ninth plague dismantled *Ra*, the sun-god, the supreme god of the Egyptians. The gods of Pharaoh and Egypt were shown to be inept and ineffective.

Pharaoh wanted to keep Israel around and exploit them for his own prosperity and gain, but now all that he had amassed is all gone. Soon Israel will be gone, too. The story follows a cycle: a plea to Pharaoh for release, a refusal, a plague, Pharaoh relents, and then changes his mind, repeat, with each plague worse than the one before. The persistence of Moses to keep coming back is amazing. The persistence of God to keep advocating for the liberation of the enslaved Israelites is stunning. The persistence of Pharaoh to remain hard hearted is inexplicable.

Are the plagues acts of God or warnings of God? If it is an act, then we have some deeper questions of beliefs and ethics at hand. It is the relentless assault of these plagues that really get our attention and I have to ask: *Is this really necessary?* We get it—Pharaoh is not a nice guy. Pharaoh wants to keep the status quo, protect his empire, and people, like the Israelites, are to be used up for personal gain. But are all those plagues necessary? I'm not really concerned about how Pharaoh feels about the plagues, but the impact on everyone else in Egypt seems to be hard to justify.

If they are warnings of God we have more room for interpretation and application. We often experience warnings where we suffer from the neglect of others. For example, when we experience a red tide along the Gulf Coast, it is a warning from nature. Pollution has affected oxygen levels and fish are dying off. Or consider when the economies of other nations collapse into despotic rule, generations will suffer in poverty. The net result is a warning to other nations who inevitably will be drawn in to rescue or exploit.

Maybe the most effective way to read and understand these plagues is to take it personally. What is plaguing you? That is an old phrase that basically means what is harassing you? Is it a lot of small stuff, like gnats in your ears and eyes that just get under your skin? An email; a comment; a vague insult? What is plaguing you? Is it some big stuff that sits on your chest and wakes you every morning and nags you to sleep? A health crisis; anxiety over work; or just plain old fear?

Often, I sit by others who want to unload their plagues. They share stories of children who are broken and their own guilt for not doing enough. There are the plagues of grief, of sin, of neglect, of brokenness, of greed. Like Pharaoh, plagues are the gods we have made in our life and therefore have made them our life. And, like Pharaoh, when these plagues have become our gods they will ultimately destroy us. This is harsh, I know, but nevertheless true. Only YHWH can save us from what has enslaved us.

The truth is I am not sure exactly what I am to do about this story of ten plagues. I refuse to believe that they are a nasty act of God, warning that if we do not straighten up worse will come to us. Neither, however, should they be conveniently skipped over, simply because they are offensive to our modern theology. When I come to such places in the Bible—and there are many—I find it helpful to take a step back and ask, "What is the larger story here?" Do you remember what I said at the very beginning of this series about the Book of Exodus? Exodus is about YHWH siding with the oppressed because God's work is a work of deliverance and salvation.

That is the mission of God—the *Missio Dei*. God wants to save you and me and invites us to join in that saving mission to the world. But it is not possible if you are plagued by all these other gods—Egyptian or otherwise. They will destroy you, but God will save.

Verse 3 of Chapter 11 is illuminating: "The LORD gave the people favor in the sight of the Egyptians. Moreover, Moses himself was a man of great importance in the land of Egypt, in the sight of Pharaoh's officials and in the sight of the people" (Ex 11:3).

As Pharaoh's heart hardened, Egypt's heart softened and now Pharaoh stood alone. Throughout history, we have been reminded that the difference between a people and its leaders can be markedly different. Germany was not Hitler, Italy was not Mussolini, Uganda was not Idi Amin, North Korea is not Kim Jong-il. The evil of one person can have devastating consequences for millions. In the end, there is judgment and salvation: judgment to those who have sought to crush and oppress because they think themselves god; and salvation to those beaten up and bowed down.

Slavery is still going on in this world. Literally, it takes the form of human trafficking, economic exploitation, and despotic rule. Spiritually, we are all enslaved to sin—when we bow down to all these other gods in our lives believing they will give us life.

It is time to flee from what is plaguing and destroying your life: the sin that has entangled you, the false gods that have seduced you, the power that has intoxicated you. They have plagued you too long, and God wants to do something about it.

We need an Exodus and we need it now. Only God can set you free.

Missio Dei:
To a World Reimagined
Exodus 12:1–15:21

When You Are Marked for Life

Exodus 12:1–28, 43–50

We come to a place in this biblical journey in which the mission of God is inviting us to reimagine this world into what could be. That alone is a thought worth lingering over. We spend so much time, I think, lamenting how the world is today: broken, a mess, falling apart…We are not hurting for examples. We experience this personally. Our families and our very lives at times reflect just how bad things can be around here. There is a divorce here, a failing grade there, an aging parent, a disappointing job.

Many churches will mark the death of a member by displaying a rose. For someone, somewhere, that solitary rose reflects broken worlds and dreams. Someone has buried their future and can hardly imagine anything different than grief and loneliness. The mission of God calls us to this broken world and calls us to broken lives, but it also invites us to reimagine this world as to what could be.

In this story, God is calling for a new and fresh start. God is calling on Israel to reimagine their lives and this world. The time of darkness is passing and life, new life, begins again.

"This month shall mark for you the beginning of months; it shall be the first month of the year for you" (Ex 12:2). Think of it as a kind of "New Year." Technically speaking, Passover is not the Jewish New Year. The Jewish New Year is Rosh Hashanah, marking the creation of the world. It comes in the fall. It is the New Year for Creation. Passover marks a New Year for Israel as God's treasured people.

The Jewish calendar is set by the moon, which means each year the month and day is different. It is said that Israel counts by the moon, "Because the moon, unlike the sun, waxes and wanes, nearly disappears and then grows bright again. So the Jewish people go through cycles of prosperity and suffering, knowing that even in darkness there are brighter days ahead."[1] Moses is told to look up and see the sliver of the moon becoming full and have hope for redemption.

Passover, by contrast, is observed at sundown in the spring of the year. This is when minds are already thinking about renewal. "This month" was originally called *Abib*, which literally means, "when the ears of barley ripen." Today it is known as *Nisan*.

The creation of a calendar may seem to us no big deal, but for these enslaved ancients it was their first great act of revolution; their imagining of freedom. A slave does not keep time. Someone else controls the calendar. Someone else tells them what to do and when to do it. One of their first acts of freedom is claiming and naming their time and their time is set by God.

The unfolding scene is archaic and gritty. First, they are told to find a sheep for sacrifice. Some Jewish sages see the lamb as a symbol of idol worship in Egypt and so its public slaughter was a repudiation of idolatry—it is a rejection of the cultural idolatry that in part has held Israel captive. The sheep has to be without blemish and provisions need to be made for those too poor to have their own animal for slaughter—everyone should have an opportunity for God's generosity. The sheep or goat must be roasted, organs and all. The meat is eaten along with unleavened bread—in the Hebrew it is called *matzah*—and bitter herbs, which could refer to the bitter lettuce grown in Egypt at the time or horseradish, which many Jewish homes use today while observing Passover. All this is to be eaten while standing up holding a staff, with "your loins girded." The traditional clothing was a flowing shirt-like garment that was tightened by a sash wrapped around the waist, which one would do when greater maneuverability was called for. Israel, you see, needs to be ready to make a move. Bread has no time to rise; the meal is to be eaten on the go. Soon and very soon Israel needs to be ready to make their move.

The air is tinged with a dark anticipation of the plague that will wipe out a sizeable population of Egypt. It is hard for us to appreciate how central the Passover is in Jewish thought. Many years ago in Atlanta, I was acquainted with a city councilman who was Jewish and one year he honored me by inviting me to his home for Passover. It was touching to see this family both playfully, yet dutifully, prepare and share in this tradition that goes back to ancient days.

In Jesus' day, the centrality of Passover was evident in each Gospel. We know, for example, approximately how long Jesus taught and served because of the number of Passover celebrations referenced in the Gospel of John. It was at Passover where he ate his last meal with the twelve disciples. It was at this Passover meal where Jesus shared with us the words that we remember when we serve communion: "This is my body…This is my blood…" (Mk 14:22,24).

In ritualized fashion, Israel is being instructed to remember something that as of yet has not happened. They are still in Egypt and there is a Red Sea they have to get through. In time their deliverance will be a memory, but right now it is just a hope. They are being asked to reimagine their world from what it is to what it could be.

You and I gather in that same kind of tension. Every Sunday we are invited to remember God's fidelity in the past, but we also gather in our present fear and brokenness and sin and are invited to imagine God's deliverance. We dwell always in the liminal space of *now* and *not yet*. Now we see the building clouds of threat and darkness. *Now* there is chaos and uncertainty. Now we battle the fear of our own Pharaohs. They have names.

In between now and not yet, Israel is told to mark their doors with the blood of the lamb. The blood holds a dual and perhaps contradictory meaning. When we think of blood, our mind often goes to death and in this context it forebodes death from the impending plague. But blood also symbolizes life and is sacred for the Israelite. Blood was to be handled reverently. The blood on the doorpost is a reminder of the life within the home itself.

Mark the doorposts Israel—God is about to do a powerful act in your life. The moon is waxing; light is on the increase; God is about to set you free. This Passover is about now and not yet. And so is all of life. These doorposts are marked for safety in the midnight of chaos and crying.

The reason we keep repeating these stories from one generation to the next is because this world needs to be reminded that bondage and slavery and oppression are enemies of God. It is not what God imagined for this world and we are being called to reimagine something different than where we are. And so we followers of Jesus have come to call the Risen Christ the Passover Lamb, without blemish, slaughtered, and yet alive to set us free. Those marked doors are reminders to the people of God that God wants to mark you for life.

God Wants to Mark Your Time

To be marked for God, Israel had to come up with a whole new calendar. The irony is that for many of us our calendars are the taskmasters that have us enslaved. Ask any young family what is going on in their life on any given week: there is ballet practice on Mondays, soccer on Tuesdays, church on Wednesdays, football on Thursdays, games on Fridays. Some of you may get to eat only one meal at home this week as a family, because most of them are on the go.

Church only adds to the competition of your time. In one of my pastorates, I asked our scheduling assistant how many events we scheduled the previous year at church. Out of 365¼ days, we crammed in 4,347 events, and that is not counting Sunday school, which meets every Sunday. If you add all of the groups that meet every Sunday morning, that number rises to 7,035. If you are bored at this church it is not because of the lack of things to attend! These are all *our* choices. Israel did not have that freedom before Passover. As God redeems Israel's time, so God wants to redeem our time, too.

The schedules cannot claim us. That is something only God can do. As trite as it may sound, God wants to be Lord of your time. It is the difference between being guided by a calendar that begs to be filled with one more thing or guided by a compass, which will help you discover where you are and where you are going. God wants to mark your time that you may know better where you are and where you are going.

God Wants to Mark Your Loyalties

We are told later in this story that Israel had been slaves in Egypt for four hundred thirty years (Ex 12:40). Pharaohs came and went and all of them demanded the loyalty of the children of God.

As I have said in previous messages, there are all kinds of Pharaohs out there competing for your allegiance. From politics to commerce to self-centered materialism, we are not wanting for a Pharaoh. God wants to mark you differently.

God Wants to Mark Your Family

In the final verses of our passage, this is anticipated, "And when your children ask you, 'What do you mean by this observance?'" (Ex 12:26). The people of Israel are told to teach them; to teach the next generation.

In our impatience we want to just tell our children what to do, "just because." Here we are reminded that what the next generation wants is to know is what does all of this mean? They want meaning, not merely facts or information or ritualism. God wants to mark your families because our children need orientation and not just another thing to buy or thing to do.

Through ritual, we practice this over and over again. We hold babies for dedication; we rise up out of baptismal waters; we embrace during marriage vows; we hold the hands of dying loved ones; we lay on hands for ordination; and we bow heads in prayer—all because we have been marked.

God Wants to Mark You for Life

It can only be so if YHWH is God, for above him there is no other. Once a colleague was sharing with me during staff meeting about the importance of breath prayer in his life. "Lord Jesus Christ, Son of God, have mercy on me a sinner." In conversation, he shared with me that praying the breath prayer, or Jesus prayer, is important for him personally because he finds if he does not pray throughout the day then prayer will only be part of his day. Praying through the day is a way for God to become his day.

It is time to mark the doors of your heart not with death, but with life. The God of Abraham, Isaac, and Jacob wants to claim you. The God of Jesus, the only begotten Son, wants to save you. The God of our calendars wants to free you. The God of this universe wants to mark you now and forever.

[1] David L. Lieber, editor, *Etz Hayim: Torah and Commentary* (New York: Jewish Publication Society, 2001), 380.

The Costly Side of Salvation

Exodus 12:29–42

Few stories in the Bible have caused me to struggle more over its implication and meaning as this story of the tenth and final plague—the death of Egypt's firstborn. I have consulted the writings of rabbis, Mennonites, Catholics, German theologians, end-time fundamentalist Christians, and some of the ministers whom I work alongside. No one has provided a satisfactory answer as to the implication and meaning of this plague commissioned and authorized by God.

I know this is a story about ethical passion. I know this is a story of deliverance. I know this is a story of God siding with the oppressed. I know this is a story where, in spite of all odds, the Israelites were saved from death. I know this is a story, like most of the stories in Exodus and throughout the Bible, about salvation. But…does salvation have to be so ugly? The firstborn of Egypt became a sacrifice for Israel's salvation. In so many words, the oppressed became the oppressor.

Maybe we can try to explain some of this away. The term "plague" for example is most often used for disease. Perhaps the ethnic Egyptians suffered some disease that affected them but not the Israelites. Or maybe this can be explained politically. All of this death is a result of the consequences of Egypt's despotic ruler Pharaoh. Citizens die all the time, after all, because of the decisions and actions of their leaders. North Korea, Liberia, and Syria are some examples of suffering and death due to its leadership. For that matter, most every war of any time has innocent or sacrificial victims. We try to sanitize them by calling this death "collateral damage" but that is of no comfort to a mother or father holding the corpse of their child.

When the atomic bomb fell upon Hiroshima and another upon Nagasaki, World War II was now over, but what about the cost? When Saddam Hussein was driven out of his despotic rule over Iraq, the people were finally free. The war itself, however, cost the lives of thousands of innocent people. I could go on and list most every war with examples of the death of innocents. Liberation and justice may come, but always with a cost that others will bear.

Is this divinely sanctioned and initiated infanticide? Whatever it is, it is a reversal of things. As Egypt called for the death of the firstborn Hebrews, now the Egyptians are confronting the death of their own firstborn.

There is no explaining this away. Salvation has an ugly side…a costly side. To ask if this is an act of God is not the point of the story, although any thinking person cannot help but question it. There is no question that innocent life suffered because of the tyrannical refusal of Pharaoh.

This story is a dark picture of reversal. Israel, the oppressed and enslaved and powerless, is now the one empowered and free. Egypt, the harsh taskmaster and political incarnate of power, is now an empty shell of death and humiliation. In the end, it is Pharaoh asking of Moses, "…bring a blessing on me too!" (Ex 12:32).

It did not have to be this way. There was a "preferential option," where God wills the good from one generation to the next. God takes the oppression and exploitation of others with deadly seriousness because it is not the intention of creation.

Like any other part of scripture, all stories of the Bible are to be interpreted through the larger lens of the Big Story. What is it, in other words, that the Bible as a Big Story teaches us about God?

God Is Creator

Therefore, God cares about what God has made. In the beginning, God imagined great things for creation. God invited the world to be fruitful and multiply and to fill the earth and take care of it (Gen 1:27). One theologian describes this as the "Original Blessing."[1]

God is creator means that every life is valued. This includes the American citizen who can trace their roots back to the *Mayflower* and to the immigrant trying to start over; the Native American living in poverty on a reservation and the incarcerated serving a life sentence. God has imbued all human beings with the gift of being created in the Image of God. It is a good and holy gift and we should value one another accordingly.

Creation Gets Broken

What Fox calls "Original Blessing" gets distorted into what theologians have called "Original Sin." This is not just between Adam and Eve and the trickery of the serpent. This is when creation slips back into chaos, which grieves the heart of God.

We, part of the creation, do not always value what God values. Sin comes in many forms, but it always distorts God's intention. Injustice, exploitation, and oppression are just some of the ways chaos is brought into creation. Pharaoh thought he was god and through enslavement brought chaos to creation. He participated in breaking the world by breaking Israel.

But Pharaoh is not the first one or the only one or the last one. Part of the function of the collection in the Bible we call the Prophets is to name the brokenness in the world. "'What do you mean by crushing my people, by grinding the face of the poor?' says the Lord GOD of hosts" (Isaiah 3:15). Because God cares for what God has made, issues of justice for the oppressed, the downtrodden, and abused are important to God. When we sin and distort the created order, we grieve God.

Salvation Is God's Mission

There are other words we can use—delivering, restoring, redeeming, liberating—but it all comes back to salvation. When Adam and Eve are cast out of paradise because of rebellion, they are given children and therefore a future. Abraham, the father of the nation, is promised a home—even though there will first be wandering and drought and trickery and enslavement. Moses, Jeremiah, Isaiah, Ruth, Deborah, and Sarah have played a part in God's work of salvation and deliverance.

This salvation was embodied—incarnated—in Jesus. Jesus was God's mission in the flesh. There is a reason why we memorize John 3:16 because for love, and in Christ, God entered the world to save it.

God invites us to participate

Keep in mind that Pharaoh refused. It did not have to be this way. Moses asked, pleaded, and, in his own way, threatened. Pharaoh wanted no part of the risk that would be involved in letting the people go.

We are invited to be part of the work that God works. Joseph dreamed dreams; Moses was brought out of retirement. Mary and Joseph said yes to a baby boy they called Jesus. Then there was Peter and the Twelve who were given a new vocation. Paul reached across socio-economic lines and reminded us God's love does not have limits or borders.

The highest ambition is to serve and not simply be served. All generations struggle against the evil forces of privilege and entitlement. What if we actively sought to change that notion by picking up our own towels to wash the feet of others?

God Is Love

If God is not love then I submit there is not really a point to any of this, for love is the best and only motivator for decisive action. Love sends us to soup kitchens and voting booths; to rescue work in an animal shelter, to preventing human trafficking. All work of God and in the name of God must be accomplished through the ethic of love and justice. Otherwise it is just good works and noble deeds. Imagine how this world would be transformed if we took Jesus at his word when he said that the love of others is one of the two greatest commandments.

I do not exactly know how this story of the death of the Egyptian firstborn fits into what I just said. I just know that the testimony of scripture in its entirety, embodied in the personhood of Jesus, and manifested through the ages by people of faith is witness enough for me.

I have dedicated my life over this conviction: God is creator and loves what is created, but creation has turned on its head. God is doing something about it and we are invited to be a part of the *Missio Dei*. I believe this and have given my life over to this message of hope and salvation.

It is true that the salvation of Israel in this story comes with a cost: the death of Egypt's firstborn. The hardness of this story compels us to reflect that all life—including the firstborn of Israel and Egypt—belongs to God, the Creator. In time, all life returns to God.

One rabbi writes in his blog: "Let us take steps to see that all of our children in this nation and throughout the world are cared for, protected, and loved. Let no child go without health care, no child go to bed hungry, no child, anywhere be denied the opportunity to grow in health and in freedom."[2]

There are only two types of choices: those which lead to life, and those which lead to death. The real question for us today is *what are you doing with your life?* To reject God, as Pharaoh did, is to choose death and great is its cost. To say yes to God is to accept a holy mission that will change your life and change this world.

[1] Matthew Fox, *Original Blessing: A Primer in Creation Spirituality Presented in Four Paths, Twenty-six Themes, and Two Questions* (New York: Putnam Edition, 2000) 46.
[2] Rabbi Rob Dobrusin, "Thoughts on the 10 Plagues," *Rabbi Rob Dobrusin's blog*, March 30, 2012, https://rabbirobdobrusinblog.wordpress.com/2012/03/30/thoughts-on-the-10-plagues/.

Don't Forget to Remember

Exodus 13:1–16

The power of memory. It can mobilize, inspire, and at times paralyze. Our home, like most homes, is a keeper of memories. Our house is not a home out of the pages of *Southern Living*, nicely appointed with wall hangings and furniture selected by a stranger. Our home is full of, well, old stuff, and not of the antique variety. It is made up of things from our past, or our parents' past and even our grand, and great-grandparents' past. If it is older than a few years, the chances are very good that it has a story. We love these tokens of memories and to be surrounded by them in our home is of great comfort.

Of course not all memories are good. Do you have any memories you would like to forget? We all do and you can appreciate why I will not call mine to mind for this moment. A good therapist will help guide you to deal with memories that hurt as well as claim those memories that build up. Memories hold power.

Israel is told to "remember this day" in verse 3. Later, in verses 9 and 16, the Israelites were instructed to remember this as a "sign on your hand and as an emblem on your forehead that by strength of hand the LORD brought us out of Egypt" (Ex 13:9,16).

Over the course of Jewish history, Jews took these words literally by wearing leather straps around their forehead and arm called phylacteries. Each strap has a box that contains the Torah. Today you can see observant Jews all over the world wear them for morning prayers. The straps are placed on the left arm, which for the many is the weaker arm. Rabbis teach that this is done because Israel was weak in Egypt and it is by God's mighty hand that they were rescued.

They mark their calendars with feasts, festivals, and fasts. They mark their bodies with circumcision and phylacteries. They mark their meals with unleavened bread and a kosher diet. They mark everything they own—from livestock to children. They mark their lives because they do not want to forget to remember. What is it that they need to remember? They need to remember that they are *bound to God*. In their impending freedom, Israel recognizes that they are not free from all obligations. Binding their foreheads and their arms symbolizes that they are bound to God and to God's words through the scriptures. They are binding themselves to God alone and they do not want to forget it.

Who or what are you bound to?

Israel needs to remember that everything they have is *a gift from God*. The strange practice of consecrating the firstborn was an ancient act of subversion from the dominant culture. These do not belong to Egypt. Sacrifices, human or otherwise, are not a guarantee of the future. By consecrating their firstborn, they are remembering that all life is a gift of God.

Do you see what you have as a possession or a gift?

They needed to remember that their future was in the *hand of God*. "… by strength of hand the LORD…" While Israel has a part in its destiny and a responsibility to go and act, there is ultimately an act of submissive trust.

Can you, in your daily routines, remember who really does have the whole world in his hands?

When you forget the risks, the consequences become deadly. You will live under the illusion of self-sufficiency but in truth you will be bound to other things and other people. We do so much to forget, to "narcoticize" ourselves from the past, but what we wind up doing is numbing ourselves against our future. In our consumer culture, we forget about our past and disregard our future because now is the only concern. We call it immediate gratification, selfishness, and self-centeredness.

When we forget, we find ourselves on dangerous ground. Israel, should it forget, will be no better than the Egyptians who held them captive for so long. When we recite the words at communion, "This do in remembrance," we are not reflecting words of piety, but active resistance. We remember where God has taken us and we remember where God is taking us.

Four times in this passage, the word "redeem" is used. As applied here, the firstborn of livestock and children was not a sacrifice to a demanding God but a reminder that God finds people valuable.

Remember playing hide-n-seek? When my children were little we played a version at home at night called "gingersnap." We cut off all the lights, leaving the house dark as a tomb and we'd hide. Usually our dog would be the one to find us and through his barking and whimpering disclose our location.

When you watch children play hide-n-seek, there is always one kid in every group that is good at hiding; so good in fact that they are rarely found.

Nobody likes playing with a kid like that. After all, the fun is in the finding and being found, right?

There is another version of hide-n-seek that I have heard about but have never played. It's called "sardines." The object of sardines is the person who is "it" does the hiding and everybody else does the seeking. When you find the kid who is it, you hide with him. One by one the kids find him and one by one they pack in there like, well, sardines. Pretty soon somebody giggles and gives away the location and everyone is found.

Maybe God is a "sardines" player. I am not that comfortable with the idea that God is on the move hiding from us all the time, taunting us with absence, but maybe we find God just like children do the finding in the game—by the laughter and giggles of everyone heaped together.

We gather Sunday after Sunday to do what God's people have been doing for thousands of years—to remember and remind. And, in the gathering, we find community where we love like a family. And one by one the people come by and hear the laughter and are blessed to discover that God is in the middle of the pile.

A Failure of Imagination

Exodus 13:17–14:4

I can get lost going home and that is not much an exaggeration. I am so good at getting lost that over the years I have grown rather comfortable with it. Sometimes I get lost because I am not paying attention. Other times I fail to ask for directions. When you get lost, do you ever stop and ask for directions? At the risk of sounding sexist, some say asking for directions depends on if you are a man or a woman. There is actually science to support this. According to the studies of neuroplasticity, there is research which suggests men are wired with a better grasp of spatial direction while women are better wired to remember landmarks. Therefore, women depend on directions and men rely on spatial orientation. Or…it could simply suggest men have a dysfunctional need to control all things and cannot admit when things are beyond their control!

We come to this story in the Bible where it looks like Israel is getting a little turned around and in need of directions as they leave Egypt for Canaan. Prior to their disembarking, so to speak, nine times Moses has appealed to Pharaoh to "let my people go," followed by ten plagues and much misery. Finally Israel is "let go" (Ex 13:17) by Pharaoh, but God lays out for them a curious route. If you follow along on a map, it is clear that God is taking them the long way around. Clearly there is a more direct way, so what is going on here? Is their long way around about the "psychology of geography?"

In one Jewish commentary it is written about this text that sometimes "the harder way of doing something turns out to be the better way," concluding, "When something comes to us too easily instead of being hard earned, we don't always appreciate it."[1] Maybe the long way around was a way to compassionately protect the people of Israel from more war. They will avoid the dreaded Philistines by going this safer but longer route. Yet we know war will come sooner or later.

The long way around might point to the larger truth that in any journey there will be pain and suffering. Some suffering is necessary. And while the text suggests protecting Israel from some suffering, they nevertheless will encounter hardship along the way. This is really not about geography but theology. It is not where they are going. It is who will lead them. In verse 17 and 18, the reader is reminded that God is doing the leading.

Can you imagine being in this large crowd of Israelites that numbered in the thousands, and when they get to the crossroads to Canaan, instead of going straight they take a right, resulting in a difference of hundreds of miles? Surely someone raised their hand in the back seat and said, "Uh, Moses, I think you are going the wrong way. You should head straight, not take a right. At least that is what my GPS is showing."

The failure of imagination begins with dispelling the notion that now that Israel is out of Egypt they have arrived fully in the promise. In truth, the journey of identity as the beloved community of God is just beginning. The mission of God—the *Missio Dei*—is neither a direct nor easy route. This is a story about finding direction—in Egypt, out of Egypt, through the wilderness, and even in the promise.

Looking for directions is a lifelong passage. I remember when I was a child wanting to be like my father. I listened to his words, watched his mannerism, would put on his milking boots and stomp around the house. I could not wait to start shaving, driving, and working—just like my dad. Every child looks to adults to find directions. Throughout life we wander, looking for directions. Sometimes we ask, but sometimes pride and control issues get in the way and we simply wander hoping we will get it right at the next bend in the road.

Where are you heading today, tomorrow? Where are you going after middle school, high school? What happens after you get that promotion or when your last child gets married? How do we find direction when we come to crossroads in life?

Here is something you need to know: At some point you will get lost. Every society, every culture—indeed, everyone—will at some point lose their way. We get distracted by changing landmarks and unexpected detours. Disillusionment sets in and nostalgia for the way things used to be can knock you off course. More than once, I have witnessed children who grow up within the nurture and teachings of the church, leave for college or careers and somehow never come back to church. The fastest growing religious category in America is the group called "nones." They are the "nones" because in survey after survey when asked to identify their religious affiliation, they check "none." We, within the religious institutions, are quick to say that they have lost their way, but are we any different? Our professions may be lofty, but our practices are oftentimes circuitous and aimless.

Life is continual movement from crossroad to crossroad. This is where we are with God's people called Israel. They are at a crossroads in their history and will need to decide where they will go and how they will get there and who will lead them. Because we already know the story, we can look ahead and name what awaits them:

a circuitous route that stretches their exodus into forty years;

a slave master called Pharaoh who does not easily give up;

an impossible Red Sea;

an impossible wilderness devoid of food.

Where is your crossroad? In my research for this sermon I came across a sermon I preached from this text years ago. Candidly, I had forgotten I had ever preached on it, which in itself is humbling to think that if I forget my sermons, what should I expect from those who must hear them?! I preached on this text in March of 1992 at Mansfield Baptist Church, near Covington, Georgia. I was still a student in seminary but was invited to preach at this church because they had called me to be their pastor. The sermon was "okay" but I assure you the context was a definite crossroads for me at the time. In two months, I would graduate from seminary. On the day of graduation, I would assume the pastorate of that church, which meant moving out of our little apartment in Louisville, Kentucky into a sprawling three-bedroom parsonage outside of Atlanta, Georgia. Our first child would be born a few weeks later. Of course, when I was preaching the sermon all of that was still in the future. I was at a crossroads and I had no idea how things would turn out.

We all have our moments at the crossroads where we are confronted with identity and destiny as we look ahead. Sometimes we look ahead with great anticipation. Other times it is with some dread and fear. We stand with the children of Israel on the banks of the Red Sea and wonder where we go from here.

You just got news that you will be laid-off from your career—*you are at the crossroads.*

Your wife tells you that "we're expecting"—*you are at the crossroads.*

Mom and dad are not getting any younger, there is talk of having to move them into an assisted living facility—*you are at the crossroads.*

A grim-faced physician mumbles something about "inconclusive results" from the battery of tests you have endured—*you are at the crossroads.*

I want you to know not only is the promise on the other side, but there will be promise while we are going through the crossroads and Red Seas and the wilderness.

This is a story about God's leadership for God's people. Therefore, it is our story too.

This is a story about great anticipation for God's people. Therefore, it is our story too.

This is a story about the shadowy anxieties with God's people. Therefore, it is our story too.

But most importantly, it is a story about the presence of God that never left God's people. To make this vividly clear, God leads by a pillar of cloud during the day and a pillar of fire by night. (Ex 13: 21–22) In the day when the way seemed clear, God was there, symbolized in the pillar of cloud and in the night when the way was less certain, God was still there as the pillar of fire reassured. God never left God's people when Pharaoh sought to annihilate them; God never left when the route seemed too long; God never left, we shall in time read, when the Red Sea blocked the way of escape.

The words of Roy Honeycutt are comforting when reflecting on the pillars of cloud and fire: "It speaks of divine presence that always overshadows God's people in every generation, in every wilderness."[2] What is it in your life that gives you the daily reminder that God is going before you and behind you and with you? We all need the assurance of daily presence.

The history of the Bible tells us and reminds us that God has gone before and behind and all the ways in between. Looking back since the first time I preached from the text—decades ago, 32 years of marriage and counting, two children and all the other stuff in between—I can faithfully say it is still true. Back then I may have preached a mediocre sermon...but I was right. *I still am because God still is.*

In the end, I do not really know the complete answer to the mystery of why men do not ask for directions. But this I do know, there is One who has promised to be present to us through our Red Seas and through our wanderings; when the daylight burns hot and when the night's darkness dims the way.

Where are you at the crossroads?

You may be at a place where you are at one side and God is at the other. God would like to separate that gap.

You may be in the middle of a family transition.

You may be at a crossroads of a career, or a marriage, or a grief.

Life is not about avoiding the crossroads, bypassing the hardship, denying the pain. It is about who will be with you at those crossroads and who will see you through to the next leg of the journey. Asking for directions is not as important as knowing who will journey with you.

[1] David L. Lieber, editor, *Etz Hayim: Torah and Commentary* (New York: Jewish Publication Society, 2001), 399.

[2] Clifton J. Allen, editor, *The Broadman Bible Commentary Volume 1* (Nashville: Broadman Press), 381.

The Other Side of Deliverance

Exodus 14:5–31

This text takes us to a familiar place: the flight of the children of Israel from Egypt—the oppressor chasing the oppressed; the hunter and the hunted. It is a familiar image. Yet this is not simply a story of Israel's salvation; it is of Yahweh's glory. This is who God is.

Israel finds itself in the wilderness, between enslavement and freedom. Pharaoh said, "go" but changes his mind and says, "What have we done letting Israel leave our service?" (Ex 14:5).

Meanwhile Israel looks back and sees Pharaoh's change of mind coming in the form of an army of chariots in pursuit. Israel looks ahead and right there is the Red Sea, a formidable barrier to a people of have never had a good history with water. Let's just say Israel gets a bit panicky. "We told you so. We told you that we would rather have slavery in a foreign land than to die in this wilderness. We told you so, Moses, but neither you nor God seemed to listen." People like security. Security, even when it enslaves you is easier than faith; even faith in Almighty God.

There are three insecure questions of Israel:
Was it because…? (Ex 14:11a)
What have you done…? (Ex 14:11b)
Is this not the very thing? (Ex 14:12a)
We are familiar with insecurity nipping at our heels and smothering us with fear. We have not studied enough, loved enough, worked enough, saved enough, trusted enough, and now we are bankrupt and paralyzed in moving forward. Between the past of Egypt's army and the future blocked by the Red Sea, what will we do, what will we say, and where will we go?

To these three questions of insecurity, YHWH gives five declarations.

The First Declaration

Do not be afraid (Ex 14:13): We hear this often in the theophany stories in the Bible. There are 67 verses where others are directed to not be afraid. God is saying to the people that their worst fears will not be realized. God is not working on the enemy's behalf or even on our behalf. God is working for the sake of who God is. Confronted with chaos, God is creator.

Haven't we all said or thought: if God would just do one of those miracles today, I would be strong, more faithful…I would believe. Miracles have been unfolding all around us since the beginning of time, literally, but we fail to see.

Friends, the *power* is not in the *parting* of the Red Sea. The *power* is in the *presence*. This was dramatized in verse 19: "The angel of God who was going before the Israelite army moved and went behind them; and the pillar of cloud moved from in front of them and took its place behind them" (Ex 14:19).

The interesting thing is the people of God could hardly buy into the presence of God. They wavered after the plagues; the Red Sea; the gift of manna; and the gushing spring of fresh water out of a rock. In fact, when the going got tough, Israel would turn not to God, but to Egypt.

In verses 11 and 12, five times in this small passage the Israelites mention Egypt. Their oppressor is the only name they know. No mention of the LORD. Yahweh is not named. Yahweh is not known, at least not like Egypt.

I suggest we are not so different than the ancient Israelites—we see our enemies and fail to reckon with God's presence.

Maybe that is why Israel needed a second statement.

The Second Declaration

Stand firm (Ex 14:13): This present chaos need not be met with flight or fight. They are to stand by and see the salvation of God. Instead of being shaped by Egypt and their fears and reacting (as most all of us do today); their perspective will be shaped by God. Slavery and bondage do not have to define them.

I have known many enslaved through the years. Enslaved to drugs or alcohol; enslaved to materialism and the appetite for more; slaves to the self and narcissism and what others think. We confront our slave masters at the Red Sea and only when we stand firm can we hope to find true freedom. Maybe that is why we love New Year's resolutions so much.

Years ago, the last one of my grandparents' era passed away. She was my great aunt and she lived to be 100, so her passing was met with as much a celebration of life as it was grief. On the day of her funeral we did what many people do: we came together in a family member's home and had lunch before the service. Following the meal, most of the men gathered in the backyard to tell stories and kick at the dirt and fidget in our suits. We stood between the tool shed and their old cinder block dairy barn. I looked at their faces, scarlet and weather-worn and heard again the stories of good times and tough times…these men had seen war, poverty, personal tragedies…I cannot help but wonder how many Red Seas had been confronted in the culmination of all those years represented on the packed red clay of that yard.

God said to those who meet up against the Red Sea to *stand firm*.

The Third Declaration

Keep still (Ex 14:14): This is not so much about passivity, for soon Israel will have to march across. This is about observing what God is doing for God's sake.

I am both amazed and amused at how we assume our words and actions can manipulate God. Books are sold that lull us into believing that if we just say this prayer, or if we follow these seven steps that God will do our bidding. Charismatic teachers are followed, listened to, and downloaded because they tell their audience what they need to do so God will act according to their needs.

This story is another echo of many other similar references in scripture: *keep still*. Our frantic energy will not change circumstances; our panicky piety will not part the water; and all the God-talk in church will not feed us in the wilderness. There comes a time in all of our lives, and it will no doubt be so in this New Year, where the best thing we can do when caught between Egypt and the Red Sea is to keep still. Indeed, Psalm 46:10 states it well, "Be still and know that I am God."

The Fourth Declaration

The Lord will fight for you (Ex 14:14): Now it is true, angels are not going to swoop down and carry them across the Red Sea. They still have to walk on their own feet. But they are to silence themselves and witness that their salvation comes from God and God alone. It will not be because of their words or their schemes or their formulas or their anxieties.

The purpose of this story is not so much to offer a comfort to Israel: "Don't worry; everything is going to be all right…God will take care of you…" Rather it's more to remind all dominions and would-be dominions who really holds the power, who is the One deserving allegiance.

The impact is no less needed today as we struggle beneath the voices competing for our allegiance, the powers that seduce us into thinking that if we are going to be strong, if we are going to live in security, if we want it all, we must listen to them. "Not so," God interrupts. The power is not in the chariot or the sword or in the leadership skills of Pharaoh, Moses, or Aaron. It is God. "The Lord will fight for you, and you have only to keep still."

The Fifth Declaration

Go forward (Ex 14:15): There is the witness to power, now comes the summons of faith for Israel. Who will you follow? In what or whom will you bind your trust? Because there will be other Red Seas. There is more wilderness yet to cross. Life, to be sure, is a jungle. When you and I meet the sea of impossibility, will we go forward or will we look back paralyzed by fear?

It is interesting to observe that in this well-known story, no one individual in Israel was invited to cross first. There was not preferential treatment to Moses. Their leader evidently had to stay behind. Neither do we read of Miriam or Aaron going ahead. Instead, they crossed together. They were in this together.

It is a beautiful picture of the church. The church is not about a collection of the stars, the rich and powerful, the influential and important, the elders and the established families. Nope. We are in this together. And when you are not here you really are missed.

To be sure, God does amaze us with great demonstrations that awe and inspire and boggle the imaginations. This God, however, who parts Red Seas and changes water into wine and makes empty the Cross is also working in less dramatic ways, giving us the courage to go on.

The real drama, just like in movies, is not in the special effects. The drama is in the larger story, the epic story that God is moving in creation. God will lead us on and will not forsake us when the only thing standing between freedom and Pharaoh's army is a vast sea.

Maybe this is why we love the spectacular movies like *Lord of the Rings*, *Star Wars*, or *Saving Private Ryan*; because they are telling us something about the epic journey in all of our lives. The parting of the Red Sea is only just a part of the epic saga. The rest of the story comes when you and I decide whether or not we will cross.

Since I have referenced epic movies, let me close with a quote from J. R. R. Tolkien, author of the book *Lord of the Rings*:

> The Road goes ever on and on
> Down from the door where it began.
> Now far ahead the Road has gone,
> And I must follow if I can,
> Pursuing it with eager feet,
> Until it joins some larger way.[1]

The summons of faith has been made. How will we respond?

[1] J.R.R. Tolkein, *The Fellowship of the Ring* (New York: Balentine Books, 1973), 38.

Who Is Like You, O LORD?

Exodus 15:1–21

"Who is like you, O LORD, among the gods? Who is like you, majestic in holiness, awesome in splendor, doing wonders? …Sing to the LORD, for he has triumphed gloriously; horse and rider he has thrown into the sea" (Ex 15:11, 21).

When you think of poetry, what comes to mind? Do you think about that dull literature teacher who forced you to memorize verse after verse of some dead person from the 18th century? I did not start reading poetry until I was in college, and then it was only because I was going to be graded on it. Through the years, however, I have come not only to appreciate poetry, but now maintain a rather sizable collection of books of my favorite poets. Poets are prophets and if we listen we can hear their subversive speech shaking up culture.

Most of us do not think much about poetry, let alone poetry as radical or important. Yet history demonstrates that the poets are the ones who shake up society—not military might or economic promise. The Declaration of Independence is made up of poetic words directed to the English empire stating, "we are colonies no more" and expresses ideals that continue to shape this nation. The poetry of playwright Vaclav Havel so stirred up the Soviets that he spent multiple stints in prison. His plays and poetic words of hopeful revolution placed him as a central player in the Velvet Revolution that helped bring democracy to the Czech Republic. It was the poetic speech of Martin Luther King, Jr. who rallied a nation to "have a dream" for a greater hope than the way things are.

The Bible is largely made up of poetry. The Psalms, Wisdom literature and the Prophets are mostly poetry, much of it dangerous. The poetry of the Bible is so distrusted and feared that it is a banned or censored book in many countries around the world including North Korea, where being caught with a Bible outside of the permission of the government can get you imprisoned and distributing it can get you executed.

Why? In part, because poetry can be dangerous. In our text today, we have one long poem…two actually. One poem is by Moses and one by his sister Miriam. According to Walter Brueggemann, this poem is recognized as "one of the oldest, most radical, and most important poems in the Old Testament."[1] Both Moses and Miriam are singing the same song: Mighty Egypt has drowned before Almighty God. It is YHWH, and YHWH alone, who has set them free. How can they keep from singing? Their song, their poem, is their credo. That is, it is a song that defines where they have been and where they are going.

Songs are poems. Do you have a song that in some way is *your* song; a song that defines you or at least that you would like to define you? I posted this question on Facebook and I had over one hundred responses of how poetry through song has made an impact. Some responses were pious: "Blessed Assurance," "In the Garden," "Amazing Grace." Some were contemporary: "My Redeemer Lives," "Christ Alone," "Man of the Tombs." I heard songs from Elvis Costello, Johnny Cash, Marvin Gaye, and Bob Seeger. Someone shared with me that their song is "I'm Moving On" by Rascal Flatts. Towards the end of the song are the following lines:

"I've loved like I should but lived like I shouldn't
I had to lose everything to find out
Maybe forgiveness will find me somewhere down this road
I'm movin' on."[2]

Israel has a poem, a song that defines where they have been and where they are going. Israel's life consists of *liberation from* and *entry into*. God, in history, is setting them free and inviting them into new life.

We see this theme repeated over and over again from Genesis to Revelation: Adam and Eve; Cain and Abel: Abraham and Sarah; Joseph; David as shepherd and king; prophet after prophet after prophet; Jesus; the disciples; Paul. All of these people and places and stories are about God leading them from a past identity into something new.

This God of history is also at work today in our history, what we call the *Missio Dei*. It is part of our Christian liturgy articulated best through baptism: *dying to Christ and being raised up to walk in new life.* We love poetry in music because the best of it is about being liberated from something and entering into something. This is the original Emancipation Proclamation, the saving, delivering, sending, and entering word.

Israel Sings Because of Freedom

Israel was defined by their slavery, and in truth they would continue to struggle with shaking that definition. Slavery and Egypt is all they have ever known and there will be times in their emancipation that they will fall back to old ways. At least here, right now, they know enough to celebrate the freedom that only God can give.

How have you been set free? In the previous chapter, I listed some of the ways we can be enslaved:
1. Narcissism and enslaved to what others think
2. Addiction and controlled by food, alcohol or illegal substances
3. Negativity and captive to self-hatred that ends up subjugating others
4. Blame and imprisoned by guilt and shame

Has God set you free? Or are you still a slave? You do not have to continue to live captive to Pharaoh in your own land of Egypt. God wants to lead you out.

The baptism covenant speaks of the ancient and continued act of God, the very mission of God: *You are buried with Christ in his death*. This includes all those things and stuff that has shackled you, entangled you, burdened you, and subjugated you. Some may not know or admit what it is that has held them captive and therefore do not yet know freedom. Take it from a guy who can never remember the lyrics, you cannot sing a song when you do not know the words.

Israel Sings Because of a New Beginning.

In Moses' song, we read:
"You brought them in and planted them
on the mountain of your own possession,
the place, O LORD, that you made your abode,
the sanctuary, O LORD, that your hands have established."
(Ex 15:17)

Israel was not just set free to do what they want and go where they will. God set them free for a new beginning.

Day by day and moment by moment, God is calling us to reimagine a new beginning, a fresh start, a hope and a promise. Otherwise, we will simply be enslaved to our old selves and former lives and never really live into God's awaiting promise and hope.

In Matthew, Jesus tells this somewhat odd story of an unclean spirit leaving a person, but coming back with seven more spirits more evil than itself. Finding the person "empty, swept clean, and put to order" they enter and live there and the last state of the person is worse than the first (Mt 12:43–45) It is one thing to be set free, but if there is no vision for a new life we are no better off than our former state. In fact, we may be worse.

We write poems and sing songs that speak deep into the human condition. We desire the deliverance that only God can give and the need for a new beginning, a hope, and a promise for tomorrow. Paul the Apostle wrote: "So if anyone is in Christ, there is a new creation: everything old has passed away; see, everything has become new!" (2 Cor 5:17).

Miriam knew the delivering and promising work of God better than Moses. She was the one that followed Moses when he was just a baby in a basket floating down the Nile. She traipsed down the bank when it floundered in the reeds; she brokered the deal with the daughter of Pharaoh that led to baby Moses' deliverance and fresh start.

Can you just imagine how important this song was to her; this ancient poem? She knew what it was like to live like a slave. She remembered the stench of the Nile, polluted with the death of Hebrew babies. YHWH delivered them from all that. How could she keep from singing? Indeed, how can we?

Andrae Crouch wrote, composed, and sung his way to heaven. Some of his better-known music included "Jesus Is the Answer," "Soon and Very Soon," and "It Won't be Long." He arranged "Man in the Mirror" for Michael Jackson and collaborated with musicians from many walks of life. Perhaps his most beloved song is one that we have in our hymnals, "My Tribute."

> "To God be the glory for the things he has done
> With his blood he has saved me
> With his power he has raised me
> To God be the glory for the things he has done."[3]

Indeed, we are saved and raised...how can we keep from singing?

[1] Walter Brueggemann, *New Interpreters Bible Commentary, Volume 1* (Nashville: Abingdon Press), 799.
[2] "I'm Moving On," Lyrics by Phillip White and D. Vincent Williams, Rascal Flatts, 2001.
[3] "My Tribute," Lyrics by Andrae Crouch, *Keep on Singing*, 1972.

Missio Dei:
A Wandering Journey
Exodus 15:22–18:27

I'm Thirsty!

Exodus 15:22–27

"I'm thirsty." Have you ever made that comment? I have this faint recollection of when I was a child and I complained to my grandmother that I was thirsty. She replied, "Well, go get a drink of water." My problem was not from lack of water. I wanted a Coca-Cola. I was not thirsty for water.

I have never really been thirsty in my life, at least not in a way where I was seriously worried about my next drink of water. When I go backpacking, I have a map that tells me where all of the water sources are located along the trail and I always pack a filter so that even if it is just a mud puddle, I can have clean water to drink. I do not want to be out in the middle of nowhere with no water.

Not everyone in this world has access to clean drinking water. Children in a church where I once served as pastor raised money for the organization "Watering Malawi," which funds building wells for clean drinking water.

Like I said, I have always had access to clean water or have planned accordingly so that I would not have to worry about serious thirst. In our story today, I can sympathize with Israel who, three days in the desert finds themselves without water. They are thirsty.

This is not the only thirsty story in the Bible. The Psalms mentions thirst often.

"As a deer longs for flowing streams, so my soul longs for you, O God. My soul thirsts for God, for the living God" (Ps 42:1–2). Jesus said blessed are you when you hunger and thirst for righteousness (Mt 5:6). He also said when someone is thirsty and you give them something to drink, it is as if you have done it to him (Mt 25:35). There is that beautiful story of Jesus meeting the woman at the well and telling her "those who drink of the water that I will give them will never be thirsty" (Jn 4:14). In another passage, Jesus says that whoever believes in him will never be thirsty (Jn 6:35) and anyone who is thirsty can come to him (Jn 7:37). Perhaps the most poignant image of thirst is from Jesus himself. When he was hanging on the cross, some of his last words were "I am thirsty" (Jn 19:28).

What are you thirsty for? What is that longing, that hunger that leaves you aching and hurting? Can you name it? Do you even know? Maybe it is as simple as peace and wellbeing because your life seems to be parched with chaos. What are you thirsty for? Some glimmer of hope while the media reminds us that the world looks like it is falling apart. What are you thirsty for? Is it that maybe this will be the day that God will finally, finally meet you in the wilderness and give you something to drink or at least a drop or two of love and assurance?

Israel leaves Egypt in the past and along with it their illusion of security. They set out three days in the wilderness—which is no walk in the park, but a barren wasteland we would call a desert—and set up camp. Whatever map they have, it does not include water sources and they are thirsty.

That is serious. I can sympathize with their complaining. I can sympathize with Moses who then "complains" to God by crying out. The language used here, however, is not simply about complaining.

It describes Israel's overall attitude that goes something like this: "What have you done for me lately." There is a difference between complaining to God and complaining about God.

People complain to me often. In many respects, that is a large part of my job: to listen to the complaints of others complaining about something I have said or done or not done; complaining to me about their own lives and disappointments; and complaining to me about the failures and disappointments with others. And that is all okay. Complaining *to* me is okay. Complaining *about* me, however, spells trouble for the relationship. You would much rather have someone complaining to you, even if it is concerning you, than complaining about you.

Pure and unadulterated prayer holds our complaints to God. It signifies that we trust God with our anxieties. We trust God with our disappointments. We trust God with our doubts. It is legitimate to complain *to* God. The Bible, especially the Psalms and Job, is filled with honest, sincere, and prayerful complaints to God.

The complaining about God, however, speaks of a rebellion that never really believed God. Israel is not complaining *to* God. They are complaining *about* God. They are thirsty and all that they think they have for their thirst is this water called "Marah" which means bitter. The bitter water reveals their interior lives. They are bitter. Israel knows a thing or two about bitterness. That is how they are described under Pharaoh's forced labor—bitter. We have read that during the Passover meal they eat bitter herbs to remind them of their bitterness as slaves in Egypt. But here, in this story, their bitterness is not with Pharaoh, Egypt, or slavery. It is with God. Earlier in this chapter, we read: "In your steadfast love you led the people" (Ex 15:13). We also read how the ground shook with singing. Now it is soaked in bitterness; bitterness with God.

Bitterness is something you can learn to like and some of us like our bitterness. Research has shown that at birth we have an average of about 10,000 taste buds but as we age that number drops to about 3,000 and we "acquire" a taste for bitter foods. Coffee, vegetables, and olives are bitter foods many come to enjoy only in adulthood. I remember as a child I could not stand the sight, smell, or taste of collard greens. Today, I cannot get enough of them.

Do you know anybody who enjoys their bitterness? I am not talking about food. There are media personalities who are bitter with indignation and stoke the fires of anger and resentment. The political climate of our day reeks with bitterness of fear and loathing. There are folks walking around bitter because of their past or what has been denied or what they have lost. Do you know anybody who enjoys their bitterness? Do you? Do you ever throw for yourself a grand old pity party and invite everyone around you to join you in your bitterness?

Israel is at a place in their sojourn where they need to decide if they are going to grumble and complain in their bitterness and stay stuck or if they will move forward.

Theirs is a history of being called to move forward. Pharaoh's imposed bitterness resulted in Israel moving forward through the plagues, through the Red Sea, and now through the wilderness. Staying stuck in their bitterness will only result in death.

Staying stuck in your bitterness will only result in death. Go forward. Move on. This requires faith, that much is certain. This requires trust. This requires, as the text of scripture states in verse 26, action: "If you will *listen carefully* to the voice of the LORD your God, and *do what is right* in his sight, and *give heed* to his commandments and *keep all* his statutes, I will not bring upon you any of the diseases that I brought upon the Egyptians; for I am the LORD who heals you" (Ex 15:26, emphasis added).

Listen carefully...Do what is right...Give heed to the commandments...Keep all the statues... All these verbs in various ways remind us to go forward and not remain stuck in our bitterness. You have to move, especially if you do not like where you are.

This is a story that makes concrete what it means to be completely dependent on God for life. Israel is thirsty and there is a life lesson to be given through something as simple and as plain as water. Water is as basic as you can get. Water is something you cannot create, manufacture, or otherwise make. Walter Brueggemann writes: "It can only be given and received."[1] Only God has what is the gift of life, both water and everlasting life.

After the plea of YHWH to listen, do, give, and keep, the Israelites are led into Elim, an oasis in the desert. There is a church near one of my former pastorates called Elim Baptist. I wonder what it is in their history that inspired them to name their church after a place known for respite and refreshment.

Perhaps one of the more striking images of quenching a thirst comes when Jesus is surrounded at night by his thirsty disciples. They are frightened. Death is knocking at their door because along with Jesus they have challenged the establishment and have dared to suggest that God is bigger than the prevailing prejudices of the time. God is mightier than any human system of political power. That God loves the unlovable; redeems the unforgivable; and sides with the unremarkable. Rome is about to take violent action and they are thirsting with fear.

Jesus sits among his thirsty disciples and he picks up a cup and says: "Drink from it, all of you; for this is my blood of the covenant, which is poured out for many for the forgiveness of sins" (Mt 26:27–28).

You will never thirst again if you trust him with your life, all of your life. You will never thirst again if you follow him as he heals the broken heart. Oh sure, you will get thirsty from time to time. But your thirst does not have to lead to bitterness.

There comes a time in every life when one has to decide to either remain stuck where they are in bitterness or to move forward in decisive action. How and with whom we move shapes and determines our destiny. The table is the invitation of Christ to move forward with our parched lives and never thirst again. Receive what God freely offers and move ahead in the faith that when you are thirsty there will be provisions along the way.

[1] Walter Brueggemann, *New Interpreters Bible Commentary, Volume 1* (Nashville: Abingdon Press 1994), 808.

I'm Hungry!

Exodus 16:1–36

When I was eight years old, one morning I took it upon myself to leave the house and explore the vast pastures and woods of our farm. In the past, my daddy and granddaddy had walked every acre with me, but this was the first time I struck out on my own, by myself, and without anyone knowing it! I walked directly to the creek that dissected our land and crossed over to the other side. Soon I thought I should be climbing a familiar hill that would overlook the grazing pastures on one side and the creek bottoms on the other. Instead, I came to another creek—this was a surprise—and it seemed to me it was on the wrong side. It was there that I slowly discovered that I was not exactly lost, but rather confused. I had walked in a circle.

For the last century, researchers have puzzled over why we cannot travel in a straight line, especially without a fixed point. Whether walking in a field, or swimming in an open body of water, or even driving a car over a plain, without a fixed point we tend to travel in circles. Scientists and engineers can put a man on the moon, but there is still not a good answer as to why we travel in circles, even when we think we are going straight ahead. I do not recommend you drive a car blindfolded to test this theory out, but I have read that.

In this life, we wander. We make plans, draw up maps, put forth sincere intentions, but as we journey along we inevitably take twists and turns and move in circles. A disappointment here, a surprise there, an interruption along the way, and before we know it we find that we are just wandering through life.

Has your life turned out exactly like you planned it or thought it would go? Of course not. In this life, we wander. No matter how much we plan, prepare, and pray, life is not a straight line, a sure path, or a fixed way. Physicists speak of the Theory of Indeterminacy (or chaos theory). Theologians just call it life.

This is the story of God's treasured people called Israel. This is their life in the wilderness. Not only for forty years will they wander in the wilderness but for all its history they have wandered. The author of Hebrews describes the faithful of Israel as "…strangers and foreigners on the earth" (Heb. 11:13).

The *Missio Dei*—the mission of God—is not about following a plan to prevent the wandering. Rather it is to embrace this wandering life, wherever it takes us with all its surprises, disappointments, and interruptions, and to do so trusting in the presence and provision of God who has wandered into our way.

When we read this story of Exodus 16, there are lessons we can learn as we wander alongside Israel wandering with God.

Wandering with God Gives Us: Purpose for Today

You cannot live purposeful lives if you are stuck in the past looking back wistfully, or regrettably, or longingly.

In their wandering, Israel has lost their purpose and cries out: "If only we had died by the hand of the LORD in the land of Egypt, when we sat by the fleshpots and ate our fill of bread" (Ex 16:3). Their present anxiety began to distort the memory of the past. All they could do was longingly look back. We shall read that most of Israel's time in the wilderness was not a time of great faith but great apostasy. In Chapter 16 alone, the Israelites grumble or murmur no less than eight times.

In this wandering life we will find ourselves in difficult places along the way—overwhelmed with bills; burdened with the risky choices of our children; or just plain bored with life—and we look back to our past and say, "Gee, life sure was better back then; I didn't realize how well I had it." I remember when our children were babies and many well-meaning veteran parents would say, "this is the easy part...wait until they are older...when they are teenagers...go to college...marry." I now know that parenting will always be hard work, but I try not to allow the nostalgic illusion of the past rob me of the purpose of the present. One of my fellow pastors called it, "Over-remembering the past."

This is your life now—not yesterday as it was and not tomorrow that is not promised.

In their wandering, the children of Israel were lost in their present and allowed their past to paralyze them for God's greater purpose in today.

Wandering with God Gives Us: Vision for Tomorrow

The treasured people of God were mobilized to move forward, not simply move out of Egypt. In their future was a land and a promise.

Israel could not get to a vision, no matter how much Moses proclaimed the great acts of God. The children of Israel kept looking back to Egypt where things seemed to be better back there. As Israel grew discontent in life they grew increasingly discontent with God. "Your complaining is not against us but against the LORD" (Ex 16:8).

Their past—slavery—became transformed into a romantic idealization and their present became repulsive to them. In their looking back they could not see where they were going. It is like trying to drive forward in a car while looking intently into the rear-view mirror. They lost the vision for tomorrow.

It is easy to do, lose a vision for tomorrow. I have seen churches do this. Their conversations are marked with how great things were back then...in 1950 or 60 or 70. "Why can't we go back to the way things used to be?" I have no doubt that there is much we can learn from our past—both recent and distant—but the God who led us faithfully years ago is no longer behind us. God is on the move and is ahead and we best catch up.

Challenges abound. Issues emerge. Needs exist. A vision for tomorrow is the promise of the *Missio Dei*; work across the Jordan River. To lose a vision of tomorrow is to wallow in self-pity of what we do not have, of what we wish we could have. Before long we get stuck. You will not be able to move ahead in life; your church will not be able to claim God's future. Bitterness and disappointment will be our end.

The temptation is tremendous to idealize our past. Our hindsight is not as 20/20 as we like to think. God wanted the Israelites—and the children of God today—to move forward. If we are going to be inheritors of God's promise, looking back won't cut it. We must trust and believe that God will be good enough.

Wandering with God Gives Us: Provisions Along the Way

In verses 12-15, we read of the tangible ways God will respond to Israel, including what is called "manna." The word itself literally means, "what is this?"

Israel is then instructed to gather only as much as each one and their family can eat for the day. There was not to be any excess and neither was there to be any lack. The vastness of the wilderness had no room for greed or for hoarding. Each one had to trust there would be enough for everyone's needs.

What we discover, however, is that Israel believes more in scarcity than in God's provision. In the remainder of the chapter, we read that some tried to gather too much; some hoarded it; some even went out on the Sabbath to look for more.

As I mentioned earlier, eight times in this chapter Israel murmurs and grumbles about where they are in this wandering journey. There is no indication that Israel believes Yahweh can do anything for them to sustain their life and provide for their needs.

Yahweh responds by giving them bread. But the purpose is not just to fill their hunger, but to test them to see "whether or not they will walk in My instruction" (Ex 16: 4). The test was simply to trust that Yahweh provides. They will survive in the wilderness if they simply trust in the provision of Yahweh. Israel must listen, prepare for the Sabbath, don't take too much, do not hoard, look out for others. Those are pretty good lessons for us today as we not only care for one another, but care for this world: Sabbath rest; don't take too much; do not hoard; look out for others.

The wilderness of verse 10 dramatically moves from a context of privation and death to a place where Yahweh's glory appears. It was to be remembered as a sign of Yahweh's presence and guidance. The gathering of manna in light of the boundaries of Sabbath is concerned with the very fabric of the community of Israel's relationship with one another and with God.

Outside the wilderness, where the power of Egypt is still very real, we are told there is no provider except ourselves. If we want to achieve in Egypt, it will have to be on our own merits: the *right* SAT score, the *right* school, the *right* career, the *right* income, the *right* neighborhood…etc., etc.

Out here in Egypt, as one theologian observes: "The market ideology wants us to believe that…life consists of buying and selling, weighing, measuring, and trading…"[1] But in the wilderness…we must decide where our trust can be placed.

Israel still could not see that it was God who led them out of Egypt, God who led them out of slavery, God who led them through the Red Sea, and God who was going to lead them through the wilderness and into the Promised Land. But now bellies were empty and souls were impoverished. Let's not misunderstand the crowds—they are willing to be led by God. But while God wants to give them a life, they want better lifestyles.

It is an arrogant presumption that it is God's job to make our lives better, to hold us together when the market falters and turn our bears into bulls. "Oh, God," we pray, "I have these plans. Please make them go smoothly." But God is no short order cook, standing behind the counter at the Waffle House waiting for us to order our hash browns scattered, smothered, and covered. We are on a journey and need to remember that God provides daily bread—what we need for the day. No need to get greedy or start hoarding. Our manna will just spoil too (Ex 16:18). That is why Israel was instructed to collect only enough for what they would need for that day—not too much and not too little. There are enough of God's gifts to go around.

Thomas Long tells of reading an obituary of a rabbi who died in England. His obituary told of his life, how when he was a young boy, he and his family were prisoners in a Nazi death camp. In the camp, the prisoners were given just barely enough food to survive—some grain, a bit of stale bread, and a few grams of lard each week. Despite their harsh environment, this boy's family continued to observe the Sabbath. Somehow managing to scrounge up a piece of candle and a little food each week, they said the Sabbath prayers and pronounced the Sabbath blessings. Can you imagine pronouncing blessings in the midst of a Nazi death camp?

One week, however, there was no candle. So when the evening came and the Sabbath was at hand, the boy's father took some of their precious lard and molded it around a bit of string. Lighting this makeshift candle, he began to lead his family in the prayers and blessings.

His son was enraged. When the prayers were done, he confronted his father. "How could you do that? How could you waste what little lard we have to make a candle? It is the only food we have." His father answered, "Son, without food we can live for several days. Without hope, we cannot live an hour."[2]

God heard the hunger of the Israelites and God fed them. And if God heard their hunger so many thousands of years ago, God will hear our hunger today. No matter what you are facing this week—legal, financial or personal—you can make it. God is going to see that manna will be provided. This will depend, however, if we really think God is good enough.

Can God possibly be good enough for you and me? May we come to a resounding yes and be fed. Jesus said, "I am the bread of life. Whoever comes to me will never be hungry, and whoever believes in me will never be thirsty" (Jn 6:35).

Jesus promises that he is that sort of bread that nourishes and sustains. Like manna, he has come down out of heaven to feed us. But he is more than manna. When we think of Jesus as bread, we are reminded that he satisfies like nothing else. We chew on him, bit-by-bit, morsel-by-morsel, taking our time to savor each part.

I want to invite you to the alter this morning to fill up on what you are hungry for: daily bread, encouragement, hope, comfort, direction, and salvation. What are you hungry for? Let Jesus feed you now.

[1] Walter Brueggemann, *New Interpreters Bible Commentary, Volume 1* (Nashville: Abingdon Press, 1994), 813.

[2] I heard this in a sermon preached at the Mercer Preaching Consultation in 2003.

Perhaps We Could Complain Louder?

Exodus 17:1–7

I know, I know. If you have been attending to the previous chapters, you are probably thinking the same thing that I am thinking: I am tired of all this complaining. In Chapter 15, we read about Israel complaining about their thirst. In Chapter 16, we read of them complaining about their hunger. In Chapter 17, everybody is just downright quarrelsome with complaints. Israel is complaining. Moses is complaining. It was so bad that Moses names the place after their mood, calling it Massah and Meribah, which mean "test" and "quarrel" respectively.

How much complaining can one take? Moses had to be at his wits end. He cries out, "What shall I do with this people? They are almost ready to stone me" (Ex 17:4). I get the feeling that Moses is ready to stone them. I cannot help but wonder if Moses is about to blow a gasket. I also wonder just how long before God blows a gasket.

I am not a very patient person with whining. My greatest failures as a parent often came when I lost my patience to my children's complaints. The same can be said for my work as a pastor. Whining and griping and complaining, especially over trivial stuff, drive me nuts.

Could the wandering Israelites be an ancient picture of today's churches in North America? We complain too much, and the rest of the world is listening. We complain when our needs are not met, when we are not being fed, when we are not comfortable, and when we are not the center of political or economic attention. The many lists out there of why people are leaving the church or have never gone to church often include that there is too much drama in the church and people have enough drama as it is. In other words, the "nones" who are not affiliated with any religion and the "dones" who are done with religion are tired of all the complaining and whining and griping going on in the church.

We complain about immigrants taking our resources. We complain about society taking away our marriages. We complain about schools taking away our prayers. We complain about the government taking away our rights. We complain when the church is too hot, too cold, too traditional, too contemporary, too accepting, too conservative, too demanding, too tolerant, too political, and too apolitical and then we complain about our children leaving the church.

I know that many of our complaints have validity. So did Israel's. They were thirsty and hungry in the desert. There is nothing trivial about that.

Behind all of this complaining—then and now—is not the significance of the problem at hand, but the failure to believe that God is still at work. It would appear that God is only as good as the latest trick. "Thanks for hearing us when we were slaves, what else do you have? We are all grateful to you, Moses, for coming out of retirement and taking charge, but what's new? We appreciate the plagues getting Pharaoh's attention, so what's next? That was pretty cool about opening up the Red Sea so we could pass through. And that was a nice touch giving us water, then quail, then bread, but, um, we are thirsty again."

Hungry and thirsty for just one more reminder, Israel asks: "Is the LORD among us or not?" (Ex 17:7). This is an incredulous and astonishing question. It seems Israel's trust and faith in God is only as good as God's immediate service to their immediate needs. It is an ancient form of a modern problem that is consumeristic at its core. It goes like this: "It is about me and when my needs are not met according to my ways I am going to complain."

"Lord," so goes the prayer, "as long as you feed us when we are hungry and give us water when we are thirsty, we will follow you." Subsequently, God is reduced to a commodity that is present only to meet our needs and when the needs are not met the product is exchanged for something else, presumably another god more manageable.

Israel is in dire jeopardy not of starving or thirsting to death, but of rejecting God altogether. The harshness of wilderness walking brings into sharp focus that following God is not commensurate with our prosperity. God offers us a better life, not a better lifestyle. It is no wonder that the place is called "Massah," or testing.

In truth as we wander along on this journey called life, we acutely know of this testing, both great and small. Life is a test, isn't it? Israel's question, or complaint, or quarrel, or prayer, belongs to us too: "Is the LORD among us or not?"

Is the LORD among you when your heart aches with loss? Parched with bitterness? Overwhelmed with fear?

Is the LORD among us when planes fall out of the sky; cancers infect children; mental illnesses cloud realities? Is the LORD among us when we lose the game; the marriage; the hope; the grade; the job?

When I see the LORD among us through the eyes of this congregation, it is not so much when every little need is met and whim appeased, but in the steady awareness that God is present in this wilderness wandering, even when there is not a water fountain in sight.

I have seen God among us as a gentle light in a dark ICU room. I have heard God among us as a still small voice in a hopeless marriage. I have witnessed God among us in the great miraculous acts that stagger the imagination, but more often when all hope is nearly spent.

Psychiatrist Victor Frankl wrote that there were three basic sources for meaning in life: love, work, and suffering. His reflections come out of his experience in a Nazi death camp during World War II. His wife, mother, and brother all died in Auschwitz. He survived and wrote his monumental work, *Man's Search for Meaning*. He observed and wrote that even in suffering one can find meaning.[1]

In the Lectionary, Exodus 17 is paired with Romans 5, which is in part a reflection on suffering. Listen to what Paul says as we keep in mind this story in Exodus: "…suffering produces endurance, and endurance produces character, and character produces hope, and hope does not disappoint us, because God's love has been poured into our hearts through the Holy Spirit that has been given to us" (Rom 5:3b–5) Suffering…endurance…character…hope… God's love poured in.

We would rather reverse Paul's list and speak of God's love that leads to hope that comes out of a character forged by endurance and leave the suffering part out. Suffering is a topic we do not speak of that much in this country or in church. Comfort—that is what most of us seek—comfort. We strive for comfortable families, comfortable homes, and comfortable churches—not suffering. Suffering as a way of life looks and feels more like failure in our comfortably upholstered dwellings of success. Suffering is denied, avoided, or when all else is exhausted, bitterly endured. Paul, however, wrote that it ultimately leads us to character and hope and love.

The Bible, as a whole, does not promise us prosperity or health, let alone a comfortable life. To be sure, there are stories and assurances of comforting, but not much about being comfortable. We read of long seasons in the wilderness and long nights in Gethsemane. There are deserts to cross and crosses to bear. In the end, we may go gently into the night but as likely we may go with great anguish and indignity.

I am reminded of a haunting line by Dostoyevsky: "There is only one thing that I dread: not to be worthy of my sufferings."[2]

"Is the LORD with us or not?" Israel has witnessed God delivering them, saving them, feeding them, and caring for them, so how can they question, "Is the LORD with us or not?" They will learn that in this life there will be dark nights of wandering through the wilderness when hunger and thirst is part of the walk.

We are still in the wilderness, aren't we? Unanswered questions; dark nights of the soul; doubts; or just simply wandering through life—we are still in the wilderness and will be until we enter fully into God's peace.

Time and time again, Israel tested God in the wilderness. The real miracles are not the daily provisions of food, water, and protection. It is that God shows up. "In short, I believe that YHWH is with us, but that belief has precisely nothing to do with acts of magic. I believe that God is present, because I know that without that presence, I can do nothing of lasting value or significance for the justice of God's world. Period."[3]

I heard once that the wilderness is a terrible place to lose your way, but it is a wonderful place to find it. "Is the LORD here or not?" God is still showing up, even when that is the only question left to ask.

[1]Viktor E. Frankl, *Man's Search for Meaning* (New York: Pocket Books, 1997).
[2]Ibid, 87.
[3]Jn C. Holbert, "Well...Is YHWH with us or Not? Reflections on Exodus 17:1-7," *Patheos*, September 19, 2014, https://www.patheos.com/progressive-christian/is-yhwh-with-us-or-not-john-holbert-09-19-2014?p=2

Who Is Propping You Up?

Exodus 17:8–16

The mission of God—*The Missio Dei*—has Israel wandering right into conflict. Has that ever happened in any of your wanderings, even the ones you were certain were directed by God?

To see how Israel confronts conflict in this story, let me share with you some background on three characters we are introduced to for the first time in Exodus. First, the Amalekites: they were historic enemies of Israel and this becomes their first battle. They are descendants of Esau, the brother of Jacob, whom Jacob tricked out of his birthright. Remember Jacob was renamed Israel and so the dissention between Israel and the Amalekites goes way back. Some battles we fight go back to deep-seated family history we thought we could forget. It is no trivial matter to point out that the animosity experienced among some countries in the Middle East today have ancient histories of betrayal and violence.

Next, we are introduced to Joshua, who is a strong military leader for Israel. While there is an entire book in our Old Testament named after him, this is the first time he is mentioned in the Torah. Later in Exodus, Joshua will accompany Moses up to Mount Sinai and will also stand by his side in the Tent of Meeting. When Moses dies, Joshua is the appointed one who will lead Israel into the Promised Land. Before all of that, in this story we read that his first battle is with these historic enemies.

Finally, we read of Hur, but not much is said of Hur at this point in the story. In fact, not much is written about Hur in the entire Bible. Some rabbinic traditions suggest that Hur was the husband of Moses' sister Miriam, but nothing within the Bible makes that connection. This is the first and fullest story about Hur in scripture and all we know is that he helped hold up Moses' hands.

The passage has a somewhat comical feel to it: as long as Moses' hands are up, all is fine with Israel in the battle, but as he drops them, so goes the victory. To keep his hands up, a rock is provided for Moses to rest upon. Remember this guy is eighty years old, so standing for the duration of a battle is asking a bit much. Moses' older brother Aaron and some say brother-in-law

Hur, get on each side and hold up his hands, to ensure victory in the battle. Is it really that simple?

There is something about Moses' hands that Exodus will not let us forget. In Chapter 4, when YHWH calls Moses to lead Israel and Moses protests that he is not able, YHWH tells him to look at his hand that is holding the staff. The assumption is you have all you need right there in your hand. Later, Moses will stretch out his hand and plague after plague will infect Egypt. Moses stretches out his hand in Chapter 13 and the Red Sea is parted for Israel to safely pass through and, likewise, he stretches out his hand to close the same sea upon the Egyptian army.

In our story today, those hands seem to hold the balance of power over victory or defeat with their nemesis Amalek. The power, of course, is not in the hands, but what those hands symbolize. Some rabbinic sources point out that Israel's victory is not about their prowess or the magical sovereignty imbued in Moses' hands, but that the upraised hands direct attention heavenward to YHWH. In other words, it is not the hands, but where the hands point.

I am reminded of the Psalm of ascent that begins: "I will lift up my eyes unto the hills, from whence cometh my help. My help cometh from the LORD, which made heaven and earth" (Ps. 121:1–2 KJV). With this in mind, I want to ask two questions and make one statement.

Who has your hand?

In other words, who is propping you up? There is a priestly image here in this drama that should not be overlooked. Remember that Aaron becomes a priest for Israel. His helping hold up the hands of Moses is a priestly way of mediating between the people and God. Who has your hand, standing with you between the mission of God and the conflicts of this world?

There is no such thing as a self-made Christian. I am reminded of a phrase I heard throughout my time as a seminarian: "We are saved in community." We cannot make it through this wilderness, this life, this world, or God's mission all on our own.

Here is an ugly truth about me: I do not like to ask for help. I am not sure if it is pride, insecurity, or some foolish notion that I am supposed to do everything on my own, but I am lousy in admitting I need help—and that is just foolish. You cannot do everything by yourself.

Yet, in spite of my reticence in asking for help, I am here today because churches, friends, family, and others have helped hold up my hands through the years. I am here today because of the beautiful mediators in my life, who took me by the hand and held me up that I might see the Holy in my midst. When I was weary and bone tired, people have stepped in and propped me up. When I wanted to give up and give in because what I was facing seemed too hard and impossible, others came by my side and held me up. I still need you to do that for me. I know I am not alone.

As Aaron bears Moses up, and by doing so bears up all of Israel, so we too are surrounded by others who take us by the hand and hold us up before God. Who has your hand?

Whose hand do you have?

If you are trying to make it through this wilderness empty-handed, you are going to die. Not only do you need others to take you by the hand but you need to be attentive to the empty hands near you. You and I have a priestly role to hold others up, mediating the presence and peace of God to them.

Moses is weary but says nothing, and his strength begins to fail him. Aaron and Hur say nothing, but seeing his weakness, they step up and step in and take the hand of a brother, a friend, a leader. Do you know someone in your life who is tired and faltering, struggling and stressed? Are you willing to step up and step in for them?

I know that you may feel completely helpless or incompetent to help another out. Taking the hand of another in their time of need is not about saying, "I have all the answers to what you need." It is simply showing up. In the book of Job, we read of a man who in so many ways loses it all. He has three friends who pay him a visit and much of the book is filled with his friends trying to comfort Job by explaining the problem, or pointing out that Job must have done something wrong, or just simply pontificating on the nature of God as righteous. In reading Job, we will notice something about all of these friends of Job: each friend is concerned with protecting their own security of faith but in doing so they only demonstrate their insecurity. They are not doing a very good job at holding his hands up.

Yet, they were not all wrong. In Job 2, there is a beautiful picture of hand-holding:

"They sat with him on the ground seven days and seven nights, and no one spoke a word to him, for they saw that his suffering was very great" (Job 2:13). Their presence of silence was their wisest counsel. Ironically, it was when his friends started talking that they ran afoul.

Parker Palmer writes: "One of the hardest things we must do sometimes is to be present to another person's pain without trying to 'fix' it, to simply stand respectfully at the edge of that person's mystery and misery."[1] Whose hand do you have? There are people literally languishing for lack of a hand.

If you are born poor, you are more than likely going to stay poor for the rest of your life. Because of food insecurity your cognitive development will lag behind the average. Statistically speaking, a child of poverty is far less likely to have a college degree or the training for a higher paying job. Instead of me overwhelming you with statistic after statistic regarding poverty, food insecurity, and minority issues in this country, let me just state the obvious: you cannot control the conditions you are born into, and those conditions can work for you and against you for the rest of your life. We are where we are because of hands that have led us, fed us, guided us, and supported us.

If when your time comes and you stand before God empty-handed... why?

The whole world is in God's hand.

Even when our hands are full, with hands that support as well as hands that give support, we cannot forget who has us all by the hand. As I mentioned earlier, most commentators note that when Moses raised his hands, it was symbolic of the hand of God. As Israel battled, they could look up and see Moses with arms outstretched as a reminder that God is with them.

If we cast our gaze back down to earth, our enemies will catch up. Those ugly family histories full of pain and regret will drag us into defeat. Likewise, if we look only into our own hands, or our leaders, or our own notions of success and power, we will eventually succumb. My hands and your hands are not enough to face our wilderness imbued with conflict and struggle.

Moses is a reminder that our journey through the wilderness, fraught with peril and enemies, can only be made when we look up and see the hand that guides us and holds us.

My friend Bruce Morgan was, for more than three decades, the pastor of First Church Griffin, Georgia. He tells the story, that back in 1882, the church's steeple was struck by lightning. During the repair, the workers discovered that on the tip of the steeple—a lightning rod—was a hand pointing upward. Over time, it was so corroded that members on the ground did not see and forgot about the hand pointing heavenward.[2]

We need people in our lives and all around us reminding, pointing, and holding our hands, showing us a better way, a higher ground, a heavenward calling, singing a reminder, "He's Got the Whole World in His Hands." That is who Jesus Christ is for you and for me. The One who takes us by the hand to show us the way and in him we find truth and life.

A benediction, properly spoken, involves holding the hands up, speaking words for God to bless the departing congregation. As we go, in so many words, we are reminded to go with God. Let us raise our hands and make certain our hands are holding others so that together, with God, we will make it through.

He's got the whole world in his hands, which means God has your hand, too.

[1] Parker Palmer, *Let Your Life Speak* (San Francisco: Jossey-Bass, 1999) 63.
[2] Bruce Morgan, *Lord, Lift Me Up...* (Macon GA: Nurturing Faith Inc., 2012) vii.

You Cannot Do This On Your Own

Exodus 18:1–27

Are you a busy professional, where every moment is spoken for and as you sit here patiently enduring an hour of worship you are already thinking about "getting ahead" of the office work this afternoon?

Are you an over-taxed mother, trying to do it all: balance a career, maintain a healthy marriage, and be available to your children?

Are you a student, tense and stressed over friendships, schoolwork, and answering well-meaning but burdensome questions about what you are going to do next?

Overwhelmed, overworked, overextended, overburdened—these and so many other words can easily describe many of us here today. In these early decades of the 21st century, we are working more than ever, longer than ever, and more isolated than ever. Technology, which in the early 20th century promised to ease our labors, has instead increased our labors. Thanks to email and cell phones, I can now work all hours of the night and day—how about you?

Of course, some burdens we just bring on ourselves: "If I don't do it, no one else will." We are burdened with the idea that the future of humanity hangs in our balance alone. In the end, we just feel overwhelmed.

Speaking of being overwhelmed, our reading from Exodus has us wandering back to Moses, who is now confronted with the overwhelming task of helping his fellow Israelites live together on this mission of God. Moses, at the age of 80, ought to think about slowing down…just a little bit anyway. From a shepherd to revolutionary leader, Moses can easily be described as the Bible's hardest working man. Even though he has succeeded in liberating the Israelites and leading them out of Egypt, his job is far from over. The people are still on a march of sorts and as their numbers grow, so grow the complexity of their internal problems of organization and cohesion. This has Moses working from daylight to dark.

In verses 15 and 16, we read that people come to Moses from morning to evening because:

1. They want to know more about God

2. To settle disputes
3. Teach ("make known") statutes and instructions of God

Moses wants to make things right with his fellow Israelites. Generation after generation, they have only known that they were property to an empire, bent on exploitation. It is important to point out that we never read of Egypt's concern for justice. Moses wants to make things right, and, as the spokesperson for YHWH, he is concerned with giving Israel not what they deserve but what they need for viable life together. But Moses is so consumed by it that he is overworked and burdened with doing good and trying to make things right.

In this chapter, we are re-introduced to Jethro, Moses' father-in-law. We first read about Jethro in Chapter 2, where Moses intervenes on behalf of Jethro's daughter, an act which lands him a wife as a sign of appreciation and covenant. Moses then is offered a job in the family business as a shepherd and he settles in for this newfound career until YHWH makes him an offer he cannot refuse.

You know the rest of the story. At this point in the reading, Jethro is back in the story and we find him checking up on Moses. Jethro sees that his daughter's husband is working himself into an early grave. He asks in verse 14 something to the effect, "What makes you think you can do this all alone?" and goes on to tell him that this is "not good" (Ex 18:17). In other words, you can do good, badly.

Let's personalize this story: are you trying to be all things to all people, even when what you are doing can be called good? Has your desire to do what God has called you to do become an illusion that if it is going to get done, you are the only one who can do it? Here are three responses for those of us who think burning the candle at both ends is a virtue; for those of us who are overwhelmed and overworked:

1. Ineffective: It is not the best way to accomplish a mission or task. Jethro is right, "what you are doing is not good" (Ex 18:17). Furthermore, he says, "You will surely wear yourself out..." (Ex 18:18a) The Hebrew for "wear out" literally translates as "fade away." The author of Ecclesiastes describes it as "vanity of vanities" and that life is just a breath that will too soon go back to God.
2. Inconsiderate: Everyone suffers. Moses is told by his father-in-law that not only will he wear himself out, but "these people with you" (Ex 18:18b). Some of us do not give ourselves permission to take time for personal care because we feel it is selfish. If you, however, are unfaithful

to yourself, others will suffer. Self-care is not selfish. Jethro is reminding Moses that not only will he wear himself out, but he will wear out those around him, too.
3. Impossible: No matter how good you think you are, it is impossible. Jethro says to Moses simply: "…you cannot do it alone" (Ex 18:18c). The notion of complete independence is nonsense.

The solution seems obvious: delegate! In verse 21, Moses is instructed to find people who "share his values and beliefs," whom he can "trust," and who "hate dishonest gain." Jethro says that others will help "bear the burden" (Ex 18:22).

Those are good words to those of us who are leaders. Those are good words to those of us who are feeling overworked and overwhelmed. Those are good words to those of us who feel isolated by the task at hand. Surround yourself with people who share your values. When values are not shared, you will work harder and not smarter. Surround yourself with people that you can trust. Where there is no trust, you will be stressed with having to do it yourself. Surround yourself with those who are not out for selfish gain. Surround yourself with people with shared values whom you trust who are not out for selfish gain. Now that is a pretty good crowd to run around with.

Moses knows that Israelites can be fickle and full of complaint. For three chapters we read of their complaints about water and food and leadership and God. Jethro reminds Moses, when you look to this imperfect people to help share the burden, find those who share your values; find those whom you can trust; surround yourself with those that are not out for selfish gain.

This is a model we see repeated over and over again in the scriptures. Jesus, the Son of Man and the Son of God chose 12 disciples to share the burden. In addition, Jesus commissions other followers to go out in his name to do the things that he would do: proclaiming and healing and liberating (Lk 10). The Apostolic Church of the first century organized seven "table servants" to share the burden (Acts 6). Later, the office of deacons and elders was established among the early churches to share the burden of doing God's work in this world. More than once, Paul reminds us in his letters to churches that everyone has a gift for the greater good of the community, that all may share the load (Rom 12:6).

Recently, I read that one of key traits that helped distinguish homo sapiens above other species was the ability to organize groups of people for a common task, but that is still limited to about 150.

We are saved in community. God has called us together to work together, seek truth together, serve together, and bear each other's burdens together. God has also commissioned us to make right in this world that which has been made wrong. Justice is not a matter of personal rights, but mediating on behalf of those who have lost their rights.

"Let him who cannot be alone beware of community… Let him who is not in community beware of being alone… Each by itself has profound perils and pitfalls. One who wants fellowship without solitude plunges into the void of words and feelings, and the one who seeks solitude without fellowship perishes in the abyss of vanity, self-infatuation and despair."[1]

The early church took this literally. In what may be described as a survivalist act, the early church members sold everything, pooled their assets, and held all things in common (Acts 2:44). We no longer sell everything and share the financial or physical load in that unique way. Yet we still have a responsibility because no one of us can take on the *Missio Dei* on our own. We lobby public servants to ensure the least of these are cared for. We roll up our sleeves and work with others to feed the hungry in our midst and counsel the distressed that come our way. We join our voices in righteous indignation when we witness bigotry and oppression.

This is why the table is the center in most houses of worship: to remind us of our common investment. We come to the table to remember that Christ has come to share our burden, to do for us what we cannot do for ourselves. Bread and cup are the symbols of sharing that we are in this life and in this community together. The table calls us back to awareness that we cannot do this all alone. The table that Christ has set in this church and in our hearts is large and inviting because we are to share in this together.

[1]Dietrich Bonhoeffer, *Life Together: The Classic Exploration of Faith in Community* (New York: Harper & Row, 1954), 77.

Missio Dei: A Covenant for Life
Exodus 19:1–24:18

Mountaintop Experience

Exodus 19:1–25

When Amy and I were newlyweds, we decided it was time to see just how rock solid our marriage really was, so we planned a camping trip. From Rome, Georgia, we mapped a route to Yellowstone National Park. After investing in a $25 pup tent and a few essentials (what they were exactly I do not remember) we headed west. While there are many details that have faded along with our photographs, I vividly remember our drive in Colorado when we first caught a glimpse of the Rocky Mountains. We were literally hours away from those mountains, but that view solidified our purpose and mission. There is just something about camping in the mountains that makes the journey to get there worth it.

Today we are going on a camping trip with Moses and his little band of freed slaves. Well, this is no little band and this is no ordinary camping trip.

If you are reading ahead, you may be thinking, "Why don't we just skip Chapter 19 and go on ahead to Chapter 20, where we encounter the familiar Ten Commandments? Isn't that what really counts?" There does seem to be a public and popular fixation with the Ten Commandments. Jews and Christians alike claim them, display them, and promote them.

Like so much in Exodus, there are no shortcuts in the wilderness; not even to get to the Ten Commandments. For the treasured people of God, relationship comes first. The commandments come second. There will be time and attention soon enough for the commandments, and not just the top ten. In the Torah, we will read of no fewer than 613 commandments. Before commandments, however, God first establishes a *relationship* before establishing the *behavior*.

This still holds true today. We can impose upon others the good words of God that are commonly called the Ten Commandments, but to do so isolated from a relationship with God is a shortcut that leads to nowhere. God wants a relationship before a religion.

All of this comes together while on this camping trip where something BIG is about to happen. Israel is in the wilderness Sinai and we are told in the second verse that they camped in front of "the" mountain. This is no ordinary mountain. This is Mount Sinai. Of course, Israel does not know what a special place this is going to be. I wonder if they think this is just a mere rest stop along the way. In fact, we are all going to set up camp at this mountain for the rest of the book of Exodus. Should you keep reading past Exodus, you will stay at this mountain through Leviticus and into the tenth chapter of Numbers. Israel will not start wandering again until Numbers 10:10, a year and two months later. At this particular place in Exodus, at the foot of the Mountain of God, we find ourselves right in the center of this very book.

It is quite a view. Looking back, we see the *call* and the *liberation* of God. Looking ahead, we will see the *promise* of God. Right here we experience the *claim* of God.

While Israel is at rest, setting up camp and pitching tents, Moses goes up the mountain to be with God. In fact, for the rest of this chapter Moses is going up and down this mountain. Most of us nature lovers have an affection for the mountains and claim to feel closer to God when we can be on or at least near them. This mountain, however, has an air of danger to it. In this chapter, the people are told to prepare themselves for this holy meeting with God. The people are to "consecrate" themselves, wash their clothes, and set limits on where you can go and cannot go (Ex 19:10,12). Walter Brueggemann reflects that we trivialize mountaintop experiences as "romantic opportunities for religious self-indulgence." In contrast, on this mountain is a portrayal "of holiness as a dangerous meeting place that will leave nothing unchanged."[1]

In other words, if we are going to go any further with God, there will be a meeting that will change *everything* and *everyone*. Encounters with God rarely reinforce old ideas and ways of thinking and relating. On this mountaintop, like that of Jesus with Peter, James, and John, transformation takes place.

On this mountain of God, Moses hears from God and is told to remind the people of God's claim. "I bore you on eagle's wings and brought you to myself" (Ex 19:4). This is an interesting image that we hear elsewhere in scripture, including the Psalms and Isaiah. Ironically, in the book of Leviticus, we are told that not only is the eagle an unclean animal to eat, but that it is an abomination. Here, it is a positive image of God holding Israel up.

YHWH then speaks to Moses in the language of a covenant; a promise of relationship: "...if you obey my voice and keep my covenant..." (Ex 19:5a).

There are all kinds of covenants in our collective experience. A subdivision, or neighborhood, can have covenants that regulate everything from the kind of grass you can plant to the color of paint on your house. Marriages are bonded by covenants. There are covenants of agreement regarding work. Here, the covenant is conditioned on fidelity to God and God alone.

If Israel agrees to live in covenant with YHWH, God will claim Israel as the "treasured possession" (Ex 19:5). We often hear Israel described as the chosen people of God. We use that term because in the Bible there are references that God chose Israel for a distinct purpose. The phrase used most often, however, is "treasured possession."

When we hear phrases like chosen and treasured, it is easy to interpret this as God has favorites. This language of chosen and treasured was adopted in the New Testament to describe God bringing Gentiles—that is non-Israelites—to share in this familial claim. Terms like chosen and treasured are not about privileged status, but inherit responsibilities. Notice what God says to Moses in verses 5 and 6: "Indeed the whole earth is mine, but you shall be for me a priestly kingdom and a holy nation" (Ex 19: 5–6). You are treasured because you have a responsibility. A priest is a mediator to others of God's holiness. Israel has the responsibility to mediate—to reveal, to shine—the holiness of God to the world. *If* they obey the voice of God and keep God's covenant.

This story comes at a pivotal point in Israel's journey with YHWH. As I said earlier, Chapter 19 comes at the center of the book's story. They have experienced hardship and now liberation. They are invited into worship, that is, intimacy with God, but this comes with conditions! I know we do not like to think of God as having conditional relationships, but that is precisely what is going on here and elsewhere in this epic story. "If you obey…and keep…" The implication is that if the children of God cease to listen and keep covenant, they cannot presume their treasured place.

Let me return to where I started. God is interested in relationship first, commandments second. In the middle of our passage is God's claim: treasured possession. Not what Israel will possess, but what God has entrusted first in relationship, second in behavior, and ultimately in trust or stewardship. God establishes the relationship and then gives the law.

Israel is reminded that God is the source of the liberation; "…bore you up on eagles' wings…" (Ex 19:4). As such, the covenant is one of social justice. They are to be priests to the world, mediating the Holy God who comes to set the captives free.

1. "obey" YHWH's voice
2. "keep covenant"
3. Then you will be a treasured possession.

Relationship with God

The Law (the Torah) will not save. Too often it seems we insist to others that in order to get to God you have to get all your beliefs lined up correctly. This story, as well as the whole of Exodus, just does not support that. It starts with belonging and the language used here is covenant. Jesus came as God incarnate giving flesh to salvation that comes by way of relationship.

Relationship with Neighbor

As a kingdom of priests, they are to be a serving nation not a ruling one. As priests, they mediate the presence of God to the kingdoms of the world. The Law is inherently concerned with neighborliness. It is not about being a better you (although it will make you better). It is about how to live with the "other" in mind.

Notice how many times God made this point in the Ten Commandments: Do not bear false witness against your neighbor. Do not covet your neighbor's house. Do not covet your neighbor's spouse. When it is the day of rest, make sure that all of your neighbors—your family and everything and everyone else—get to rest just like you do. And, oh yes, the elderly—"your father and your mother"—are still your neighbors as well.

Paul makes the same point in Galatians: "The entire law is summed up in a single command: 'Love your neighbor as yourself'" (Gal 5:14). And in 1 Peter: "But you are a chosen race, a royal priesthood, a holy nation, God's own people, in order that you may proclaim the mighty acts of him who called you out of darkness into his marvelous light" (1 Pet 2:9).

The missional impetus of the New Testament finds its inspiration from the Old Testament.

These words are for free people. God has set the people free because that is who God was then.

And that is who God is now. God has come to set you and me free.

---

[1] Walter Brueggemann, *New Interpreters Bible Commentary, Volume 1* (Nashville: Abingdon Press, 1994), 837.

Ten Words to Live By

Exodus 20:1–17

Do you have a "favorite" or "go-to" commandment? Most societies recognize the importance of not murdering, stealing, or bearing false witness. Pretty basic stuff. In fact, many commandments are found in an earlier document called the "Book of the Dead," which has Egyptian origins. What about commandments you conveniently ignore or count as a suggestion instead of a commandment—let's be honest now. Keeping the Sabbath holy? Dubious in our 24/7 culture. Or what about the one about not coveting—imagine what would happen to our economy if we rejected consumerism's pull for more and better and faster.

We love talking about the Ten Commandments, don't we? We print them, recite them, post them, make jokes about them, and ask others to display them, whether they believe in them or not. There are monuments erected throughout this country displaying the Ten Commandments, which is a bit ironic considering the second commandment is against graven images.

Jews refer to them as the "Ten Words" or *Decalogue*, and they number them slightly differently than Christians, counting verse 2 as the first commandment instead of verse 3. Catholics and Lutherans have a different listing as well. As a whole, we all share the same list of commandments, but there are differences in the ordering according to religious background and depending on if you use Exodus 20:1–17 or Deuteronomy 5:6–21.

The Ten Commandments should actually be called the "first" ten commandments. There are more than just ten, 613 to be exact, which Jews refer to as the *Mitzvot*. I suspect, however, most of us cannot even recite all ten of the "top ten," let alone remember the other 603.

Comedian Jay Leno once challenged bystanders to name one of the Ten Commandments for "The Tonight Show." The most popular answer? "God helps those who help themselves." Not only is that not one of the commandments, it is not even in the Bible. In similar fashion, several years ago, Stephen Colbert interviewed a congressman from Georgia who was sponsoring a bill to display the Ten Commandments in the House of Representatives. In the interview, Colbert asked him to name the Ten Commandments. After a moment of uncomfortable fidgeting, the congressman said: "Umm...don't murder...don't lie...don't steal." After naming just three he said, "...umm I can't name them all." As an added dig, Colbert closed the interview by saying, "Congressman, thanks for taking time away from keeping the Sabbath holy to come talk to me."

I wonder how most of us really, really feel about the notion of "commandments"? To begin with, not many of us want to be commanded to do anything. It sounds subservient, domineering, and demeaning. What would it be like for you to show up at a staff meeting and your boss say, "I command you to get those sales numbers up?" How would it sound to you if your spouse told you, "I command you to prepare meatloaf for dinner tonight"? Do you know any teenagers who would react well to being commanded to clean their room, make good grades, or choose better friends? No one wants to be commanded to do anything, even good things.

Does the word "commandment" sound like a burden or blessing? I suspect you know the right answer is blessing but deep down it feels more like a burden.

"Thou shalt not...!" To make it sound more emphatic we remember the Ten Commandments in the old King James Version. Thirty-six times in Exodus alone, God is reminding the Israelites what they "shalt not" do.

Let me be candid: we do not like being told "no." That is one of the first words we learn to speak—no—implying through the understanding of a two-year-old that "I will do what I want to do." After all, we are told throughout life that "the sky is the limit" and "you can be whatever you want" and "if it feels good do it" and "if you want it take it." From credit cards to automobiles, we are sold into thinking that if we want it we can have it if the price is right.

One of the great struggles facing churches throughout North America is that we see ourselves less as a shared community—what the early church called "koinonia"—and more as a gathering of individuals where the customer is always right and where we come to have our personal needs met. Being told "no" is something many of us, even in the church, just do not like to hear.

God said...*no*. As much as I like the idea of the power of positive thinking and as much as my encouraging, life-affirming ways would like it to sound otherwise, these Ten Commandments, or ten words as our Jewish friends call them, begin with no: no other gods, no idols, no wrongful use of God's name, no to work all of the time, no to dishonoring your mother and father, no murder, no adultery, no stealing, no lying, no coveting. Just say no. So which is it for these commandments? Burdens or blessings?

If all we hear is that to be on God's mission to redeem the world, save the world, liberate the world means that we spend all our days weighted by the encumbrance of saying no, then I suppose a commandment is a burden.

When commandments become burdens, we then are at a grave risk of burdening others with them too, like a heavy granite monument sinking deep in soil. Religion becomes burdensome. God becomes burdensome. Church becomes burdensome. Church members become burdensome. And we wonder why people are walking away from the faith and from church.

The Pharisees saw the commandments as burdens and created additional burdens for others to bear in order to keep the commandments. There was an oral tradition that served as a "fence" around the commandments to protect them from being broken. In this context, Jesus responded, "… my yoke is easy, and my burden is light." (Mt 11:30).

Are you making the commands of God burdensome for yourself? What about to others? It would appear to me that many see Christians as "anti," defined by all those things and people we are against. In the 1990s, Dana Carvey created a sketch for Saturday Night Live spoofing Christians with the "The Church Lady." We laugh at such characters, but there is an uncomfortable element of truth behind the comedy.

What if we reframed how we view these commandments of God? If we see these commandments as generous acts of love both to God and to one another, then we experience these commandments not as burdens but as blessings.

The commandments begin with a *claim* and end with a *commission*. In a rabbinic commentary, the observation is made that it is "striking that the document opens with 'the LORD your God' and closes with 'your neighbor.'"[1]

The Ten Commandments begin with a claim.

"I am the LORD your God" starts the list and it is a personal word which Israel was starving to hear. In the lonely wilderness of wandering where Israel is not yet home, God makes a claim. In the Hebrew the word for "your" is singular. You are not just one of a crowd. You are a special and unique "you" on whom God makes a claim. Jews count this as the first commandment, not simply the introduction to verse 3. Notice, too, that it does not begin with

"Thou shalt not.' Neither is it really a commandment. And it certainly is not a burden.

Yet, we still bear the burden of being unclaimed, like lonely luggage lost at an airport. Three thousand or so years later, beyond the cognitive revolution, the agricultural revolution, and the scientific revolution, and in spite of technology that has given us email, social media, and FaceTime, we are more isolated and alienated than any other era in history. Increasingly, study after study is suggesting that as technology creates more bridges of connectivity we are correspondingly growing more isolated. Years ago, we thought the television was going to divide families. Now even if family members are sitting in the same room, the chances are good that they are not even watching television together. Instead, one is looking at an iPad; another is checking a smartphone; and someone else is on their laptop. We are a lonely culture living in a lonely time in spite of having connections all around the globe. Loneliness is burdensome. It is grueling. It is dehumanizing.

In the lonely wilderness, God made a claim to Israel: "I am YHWH your God." In the simplicity of a few Hebrew words it says in effect: I belong to you. It is God's claim, a claim that we cannot make for ourselves nor one that we can make for others. It comes from God; initiated, spoken, and put into Law by God. God is saying, "I am yours and you are mine."

Pharaoh and the oppressive machine of chariots and force that threaten to destroy all others cannot stand against this claim of God.

All of Egypt and any other principality or power that exploits people as objects for selfish gain cannot stand against this claim of God.

The wilderness with its threat of annihilation and privation and fear cannot stand against this claim of God.

In this world of loneliness and isolation; in this world that subdivides again and again according to race, nationality, and income, God makes the indisputable and irrefutable claim: "I am the LORD; I am Yahweh, I am yours and you are mine." There is nothing or no one that can stand against this claim.

The future of the church depends not on what kind of music we sing or what kind of pastor is preaching or what kind of buildings are constructed. The future of the church depends on how we accept this "commandment," this claim of God. Will we be a church where we can say to one another, "I belong because God said so"?

The Ten Commandments begin with a claim and…

The Ten Commandments end with a commission.

The first half of the Ten Commandments is entwined with God's claim for each of us and our claim to God, and the second half is concerned with God wanting us to claim our neighbors. By "claim" I do not mean possess but to care for our neighbors. The image of the commandments coming to us on two tablets places the relations with God on one tablet and the relations with neighbor on the other tablet. Paul the apostle knew this too. In his letter to the Christians of Rome, he wrote: "The commandments, 'You shall not commit adultery; You shall not murder; You shall not steal; You shall not covet;' and any other commandment, are summed up in this word, 'Love your neighbor as yourself.' Love does no wrong to a neighbor; therefore, love is the fulfilling of the law" (Rom 13:9–10).

Friends, this is a holy commissioning; an ethical imperative; a saving declaration that saves us from our selfishness.

A few years ago, the movie *Selma* was nominated for several Oscars, one of which was Best Original Song. During the Academy Awards that year, the song, "Glory," was performed by pop singer John Legend and R&B musician Common. Common said, "Recently John and I got to go to Selma and perform on the bridge that Dr. King marched on 50 years ago. … It was once a landmark of a divided nation, now a symbol for change. … The spirit of this bridge was built on hope."[2] I love that image of the bridge that once symbolized division now reaching over hopefully.

These Ten Commandments can either be burdens of division, and they will be if we continue to insist upon others that my way is the only way. Or they can be a bridge to both God's claim and God's commission. "I am YHWH *your* God," starts the conversation and it reaches its glory with the admonition that you are to love through these commandments "…your neighbor."

As Selma becomes the bridge for change, God's covenant was intended to lead the people from selfishness in the wilderness to neighborliness rooted in love by and from God. It was radical then and it still is radical today.

Of course, we need both tablets—the claim and the commission. We need to "get it right about YHWH" in order to "get it right about neighbor."[3] To attend to right relations with neighbor is to attend to right relations with God and vice versa.

When you know who you are (claimed by God), you know what to do (commissioned by God).

¹David L. Lieber, editor, *Etz Hayim: Torah and Commentary* (New York: Jewish Publication Society, 2001) 442.

²Sam Rullo, "John Legend & Common's Oscar Speech Was Inspiring," *Bustle*, February 22, 2015, https://www.bustle.com/articles/65840-transcript-of-john-legend-commons-oscar-acceptance-speech-proves-glory-has-a-timeless-message-video.

³Walter Brueggemann, *New Interpreters Bible Commentary, Volume 1* (Nashville: Abingdon Press, 1994), 839-840.

Do You Read the Owner's Manual?

Exodus 20:18–23:19

Do you ever read the owner's manual when you buy a new product? I am the type of guy who will pick up an owner's manual from a recent purchase and maybe glance at the table of contents, but will quickly tuck it away, never to look at it again—unless of course there is a problem. I know people who get as much, if not greater, joy in going through an owner's manual as using the actual product itself.

These chapters in Exodus look much like an owner's manual for newly liberated Israel. Technically, they are better described as a code, specifically a legal code. This passage is considered one of the oldest, if not the oldest, collections of legal code in the Bible. Scholars refer to this section as the "Book of the Covenant," which comes from a reference in Exodus 24:7. The trouble is this covenant or code has no coherent pattern, structure, or order, so it makes for very difficult reading.

Then again, most all legal code is cumbersome to read. Besides lawyers, have you ever read a legal code? It is not exactly engaging literature. I have discussed with lawyers in my church about the U.S. Code and all agreed it is overwhelmingly large, complex, and always changing. Basically, in a typical law office an entire wall is filled with the volumes and supplements representing the U.S. Code. I guess we should not complain much about three small chapters in Exodus.

Codes are needed because they give guidance on how to live together; how to define what is just and right; and they provide a sense of order and protection. Without codes or law or covenant there would be anarchy.

Most churches are organized according to "codes," usually called the Constitution and By-laws or maybe Standing Rules. I served a church that kept its constitution in a three-ring binder, and it is nearly two hundred pages in length—nothing like the U.S. Code, but then again it is not much more exciting!

Most agree that rules are necessary, but honestly not many of us like them. When I go to the YMCA to work out, right there in the middle of the fitness area is a very large sign of rules that mostly tells us what we cannot do or wear or say. Who really likes rules?

Imagine, however, living without them. Imagine being denied them. Imagine if you were a woman or child living in Saudi Arabia, for example. Floggings and executions are sadly still common in that oil rich country whose codes do not stand up for women as they do in our own country. In other countries, women and children are the most vulnerable to human trafficking because they have no voice or advocate. Just imagine living in a country like China or North Korea, where owning a Bible can get you in trouble and speaking openly about your faith can get you arrested. Just imagine what it must be like to not have a code, a law, or a covenant to watch out for you.

As slaves in Egypt, Israel had no rights, no justice, and no dignity or value as persons. They were just cogs in an imperial machine of brick making and pyramid building. What some may see as laborious codes that restrict, Israel was able to hear, "Finally, we have value. Finally, we have worth. Finally, we have direction on how to live and love and respect one another."

They have been given freedom and now they have responsibility. Eleanor Roosevelt once said, "Freedom makes a huge requirement of every human being. With freedom comes responsibility."[1]

What does this "Code" have to say to us about freedom and responsibility? To be fair and candid, this code reflects some of the difficulties we often have when it comes to reading the Bible, particularly the Old Testament. It is in so many places culturally irrelevant and archaic and, yes, offensive. Here are some examples of what this code, this "Book of the Covenant" covers:

1. Buying slaves (Ex 21:2ff)
2. Selling daughters as slaves (Ex 21:7)
3. Capital offenses for murder, kidnapping, a child that strikes or curses a parent, (Ex 21:12-17)
4. What to do with an ox that injures a man or woman (Ex 21:28ff)

The above is just with Chapter 21. This language goes on for several more chapters with the lingering smell of irrelevancy. Does any of this shape us for the 21st century living into the *Missio Dei*?

We understand that those days were different than our times. It was an agrarian based economy, not a capitalist and consumeristic one. Social structures were radically different than our modern Western ideas. Customs, society, and culture changes and, along with it, religious instruction has to adjust too. We no longer have slaves, let alone make allowances for selling our children for debt relief. We no longer execute criminals for offenses except for murder. We no longer base our laws along agricultural considerations. What then do we do with this section of the Bible? Do we rip it out? Do we skip over it as irrelevant? Do we pick out the sections we like and disregard the ones we do not?

Let me suggest that for this section of the Bible we not pick it apart or ignore it or reject it. Rather, let us look at it as a whole and see what is at the heart being said to these people treasured by God, freed by God, and now entrusted with being responsible to one another and to God. Here are some quick observations about what this Book of the Covenant is about.

The Law of God is about dignity.

We begin our reading with instructions about how to treat slaves and are no doubt dismayed there is not an unequivocal rejection of slavery. At first glance, this is startling and offensive. The Israelites, after all, were at one time slaves. While we should in no way defend slavery in our time or in any other time, three thousand years ago slavery was a reality. In this real world there is code, law that reminds Israel that all persons still have worth above commerce, therefore instructions are given for their freedom and protection. In Egypt, a slave had no voice. Even in this reprehensible system, the Law of God is directed towards their dignity by advocating rest and eventually release.

Dignity is for all persons. There are other examples. In Exodus 22:27, the Covenant states that if you take your neighbor's cloak in pawn, give it back to him by sundown because, "it may be your neighbor's only clothing to use as cover." In Exodus 23:6, the Covenant reads, "You shall not pervert the justice due to your poor." In Exodus 23:9, the Covenant reads, "You shall not oppress a resident alien," reminding Israel, "you were aliens in the land of Egypt."

The Law of God is about dignity. Without question, times have changed and with them our culture and society, but I side with Jesus who said, "I have not come to abolish the Law but to fulfill it" (Mt 5:17). I believe Jesus meant that God still cares about human dignity, even though our society inevitably moves on to other structures and systems.

Fifty years ago, marchers traversed over a bridge in Selma because they believed that at the heart of the law dignity was valued, even for people of color. What are the issues we face today that threaten human dignity? Immigration? Welfare reform? Access to healthcare? Food insecurity? I cannot faithfully say that the Bible is always clear about how to handle such political and politicized issues. Personally, I do not always know the right thing to do in many of the issues we face in our country and in this world. I do know and believe that the laws of God point us to human dignity. I can say, and believe, that Exodus reminds us: "…if your neighbor cries out to me, I will listen, for I am compassionate" (Ex 22:27).

The Law of God is about dignity, which means we are to advocate dignity for others too.

The Law of God is about justice.

Loving together means life together and so we have to know how to live together. Justice is concerned with how to live together. For example, in this passage we read the following: "If any harm follows, then you shall give life for life, eye for eye, tooth for tooth, hand for hand, foot for foot, burn for burn, wound for wound, stripe for stripe" (Ex 21:23–25).

No question that those are tough words. But look again. Israel dwelt in a time where vengeance was the law. Vicarious punishment that exceeded the harm incurred was the rule. An eye for an eye was a protest against their culture, advocating instead that there needs to be justice but there is no place for vengeance.

The Law of God is about community and therefore justice within the community is essential. Reading through these chapters we read how ox and donkeys and work and profit are important to industry, but not more important than the community. Every seventh year, the ground is to be left fallow so the poor can eat and what they do not eat the wild animals can eat (Ex 24:10). Not good for commerce but necessary for community. Every seventh day, everyone is to rest including ox, donkeys, slaves, and resident aliens. Not good for profit but justice is for people, not profits.

The Law of God values community above commerce. Because God values this, should we not value it too? Community is essential. It starts in the home and is celebrated as a congregation. We are "bound" together and therefore advocate for others. Jesus said this is especially so for "the least of these."

The Law of God is about priority.

This code includes rather arcane instructions about worship: which festivals to observe and when to observe them; what to eat and what not to eat; what to do and not do (like not boiling a lamb in its mother's milk). Today most Christians do not observe these festivals or keep a kosher diet. Why do we need to pay attention to passages such as these?

Because the Law of God is about priority; keeping first things first. This is accomplished through worship. We do this in the course of a church year. Through the birth, life, sacrifice, and resurrection of Jesus we have a model for how we are to live as a people of God.

1. Worship reorients
2. Worship restores
3. Worship reminds

This collection really is not a handbook, and I hesitate to call it a legal code. It really is a covenant of God wanting us to value what God values: dignity and justice. Worship helps us prioritize the living of our days accordingly.

No one in our immediate family ever went to law school. Outside of drawing up a will and closing on a house, I have never needed a lawyer. I know a lot of lawyer jokes, but like preacher jokes they are mostly unfair. Most of the lawyers I know are good, good people who got into the work because they believed in the inherent dignity of others and because they wanted to advocate justice for others. They work with the code that has been given to them and lobby to change the code when it is wrong.

No, I have never much needed a lawyer, but I am so glad to know that they are out there working and serving and at times saving. They do this because of a belief in dignity and the knowledge that we must live together in this country.

What will shape you in this waiting world? What will shape us for this life together? What will be our priority for the *Missio Dei*?

[1] Eleanor Roosevelt Quotes. BrainyQuote.com, BrainyMedia Inc, 2020. https://www.brainyquote.com/quotes/eleanor_roosevelt_166988, accessed August 16, 2020.

Breaking Chains

Exodus 23:20–33

God has come to set the people free. Over and over again we see that the recurring theme in the Bible is God's commitment to freedom—material freedom, economic freedom, and spiritual freedom. The first command to "be fruitful and multiply (Gen 1:28)," assumes freedom.

Have you ever had someone get in front of you to protect you, take care of you, or maybe just get things prepared, so that you could be free to move forward?

There is an echo of this passage in Mark's Gospel where that story begins: "Behold, I am sending my messenger ahead of you…" (Mk 1:2). Mark is telling us that we are being prepared for the salvation, the freedom that is to come.

Exodus 23:20 has YHWH declaring to Israel that an angel, a messenger, is sent to go in front of them, in effect, preparing the way for the salvation that is to come. Here are a few brief observations from this text:

Verse 20 says, "send an angel in front of you"—We first read about an angel in Exodus in Chapter 3. It is an angel in the burning bush. Later in Chapter 14, we read that an angel moves from leading Israel out of Egypt to moving behind Israel separating them from the Egyptian army. The angel is a reminder that Israel is divinely guided and guarded.

Verse 22 states that God's leadership and protection is conditional, "if"— There are conditions. Few want to speak about, let alone think that God has conditions, but all relationships have conditions. We expect love and faithfulness and when that is not shared the relationship changes.

Like it or not, God has conditions for Israel as this text and many others like it remind us. Life itself is a series of conditions and causes. It is as basic as laws of physics and as mystifying as the Law of God. Israel has been set free, but their freedom comes entrusted within the covenant of God. "If…" is the condition to Israel. "If you listen…If you obey…If you hear…If…" All these conditions are entwined in the covenant of God.

Verses 23 through 33 leave us squirming as we read of what looks and sounds like complete conquest and total annihilation mixed in with a little "health and wealth gospel." "Blot out" is how the NRSV translates what God will do. Israel is then told that they are to take down the old structures of idolatry and exploitation, and organize itself according to the covenant they have received. They are to, in other words, live differently. Additionally, there is the apparent promise of health, fertility, and prosperity. Yet we know this is not quite the whole experience. Not then and not now, no matter how you read history. Finally, they are warned that if they compromise their fidelity to God alone the other nations will be a "snare" to them.

Without question this text is peculiar and antiquated to our contemporary notions of God's claim of people and place.

Let's think about this story critically. Israel, in spite of its newfound freedom, is hardly a formidable foe to other, more established, civilizations. Yes, we can infer in the text that God will do the fighting, but how does that make God look? Some scholars suggest that what is to be destroyed, or "blotted out," will be their systems of governance. The Canaanite systems are based on exploitive power. Israel comes in with a covenant. They are to live together with a care for the neighbor, centered on justice for the exploited, and loyal to YHWH alone.

What strikes me most about this story is how it begins: God sends a messenger to get out in front of Israel for the purpose of protection and preparation. As we read this text, we are reminded of a recurring theme that runs deep in the being of God, and that is:

When God goes before you, chains are broken.

Just ask Pharaoh and his chariots of power; just ask Herod and his empire of insecurity; just ask Pilate and his hands soiled by indifference; just ask Rome, who built a cross that could not ultimately bind the Son of God.

When God goes before you, chains are broken. This is the *Missio Dei*, the mission of God out in the world; the plan of God that cannot tolerate chains of any kind except for those that bind up what is evil and wrong in this world.

When God goes before you, chains are broken... for your neighbor.

God cares about the neighbor, who has set us free from ourselves and the chains of self-absorption. Ten times "neighbor" is mentioned in this small section called the Book of the Covenant (Ex 20–24). "Do not bear false witness…do not covet…" (Ex 20:16,17). "If your neighbor cries out to me, I will listen…" (Ex 22:27). God cares about the neighbor.

And because God cares about the neighbor, God has set us free from ourselves and the chains of self-absorption. A contemporary icon of self-absorption is the "selfie," a self-portrait taken in front of a mirror or simply holding the camera out in front of you. "Selfies" are not very interesting if you are the only one in the picture.

Church can fall into the cultural quagmire of an institutional selfie. Small groups, Sunday school classes, and ministries can look like "selfies" that are familiar, yet lonely. Long ago disciples hid behind locked doors out of fear, but Jesus not only found his way in but, in turn, opened the doors wide— "No more selfies! Get out there and love the neighbor, the stranger, and the outsider like I taught you!" (That is the Greg DeLoach Version [*GDV*] from Matthew 28:19.)

In this life, God created us not to live as walking "selfies" but to live in vibrant community. While the phrase "Covenant of God" sounds heavy with legalism, it really is a generous invitation to save us from ourselves so that we can live more fully with one another. Life together is not a closed community of insiders against the outsiders, but a porous way of living, relating, serving, and advocating. God has gone out in front of us to break the chains of selfishness because God cares about our neighbors.

When God goes before you, chains are broken… for the outsider.

Therefore God has set us free to practice hospitality. In the Old Testament, many English translations use the word "alien" to refer to outsiders. Contextually it means simply, "you are not from here." In other places "stranger" is also used. Abraham lived as an alien and so did Israel for much of its existence. God cares about the outsider, so God set Israel free to care about the outsider too.

Who are the outsiders for our times? Immigrants, legal or otherwise count. How about those beyond your social circle or your educational standing? What about those whose moral behavior is not only different than yours or mine, but could even be called offensive? Do they count? I think so.

When God goes before you, chains are broken...
for fidelity.

Therefore God has set us free from fickle loyalties based on convenience instead of conviction. I am troubled by the deluge of statistics that are pointing to a growing interest in a personal faith but not in a shared faith; what some may call "spiritual but not religious." I understand that there are many who love Jesus but have trouble with Jesus' fan club. Still, the covenant calls on us to live into the *Missio Dei* together in faithfulness because in community we transform the world.

God has gone out in front of Israel and for us too, breaking chains and setting people free. We are reminded of the words from 2 Timothy, "The word of God will not be chained," and so we must not, best not, chain up what God intends to set free.

Yet we are always trading chains. God's words, "I will blot out" the Canaanites and all the rest is not a reference to genocide. It means God will blot out their systems of exploitation and chain forging. Otherwise, Israel is in real danger of trading one set of chains for another set.

We know that Israel will do just that—trade in one set of chains for another. They will fail and fail miserably; just like we have failed and will fail miserably. We are often moving from one set of chains to another. Victims can look like victimizers. Israel moves into their freedom as conquerors, then judges, then imperial, and back to landless—all within a few short generations.

When someone else is in chains, we all are in chains. Like the angel of old, God keeps going on ahead of us, breaking chains as fast as we forge new ones. God gets in front and sends John the Baptist who points to Jesus; Jesus points to the Apostles; the Apostles point to the church; and the church points back to neighbors and neighborhood, movements and missions. The *Missio Dei* is going on ahead of us breaking chains and setting the people free.

When we catch up to God, chains are broken and people are set free to love one another; advocate for one another; to worship together; and to live together. In this world of ISIS terror and Ferguson failures, we need God more than ever to go in front of us and break chains.

One of the most memorable stories Jesus told followed an exchange over the commandments. Nowadays, we either recoil at the thought of debating law or we settle back in polite boredom. Jesus has a way of transforming commandments into purposeful living. Jesus taught that to love God and love one's neighbor were the two most important commandments and then tells the story of "The Good Samaritan." The story ends with a surprise resolution of the outsider doing good to the one most in need, to which Jesus asks: "Which of these…was a neighbor to the man who fell into the hands of the robbers?" The answer is obvious: "The one who showed him mercy." The commissioning is obvious too: Jesus said to him, "Go and do likewise" (Lk 10:36–37).

May God commission you on a mission of mercy with your family, with your colleagues, and with complete strangers. May your "selfies" be filled with neighbors and acts of generosity and justice and mercy and fidelity. May you be free of your chains and never rest until all others are free, too.

When Awesome Really Is the Only Word

Exodus 24:1–18 [12–18]

In the late 2000s, "Cloud computing" evolved and whether you know about the Cloud or not, most all of us use it. In brevity, it is how much of our digital information is stored. Pictures on your phone, music that you listen to and data that you depend on is often stored in the "Cloud." If something happens to the Cloud, there goes your stuff. Like the radio, I do not understand the Cloud. The Cloud is a mystery to me. The Cloud is scary. I mean, where does all our stuff actually go? Into thin air?

Chapter 24 ends with Moses going into the cloud on the Mountain of God, and he will not come out for another 40 days. Due in part to the familiarity with Moses and the Ten Commandments, we often get this story convoluted. When we first read about the Ten Commandments in Chapter 20, they are given to Moses orally, not written on stone or tablets. It is only in this chapter that we are told about the two tablets. Moses is sent back up Mount Sinai, which in our story today is called "Mountain of God." Moses goes to represent the people to God and God will place upon Moses the covenant binding the people for God.

Throughout history, mountains have been designated as sacred places. One story about a sacred mountain describes it as covered in clouds, with fire burning and around it are erected twelve stone monuments. No, this is not a description of Sinai, but of Olympus, where Prometheus ventured to steal fire from Zeus and bring it down the mountain to the mortals, so they might have life.

Another mountain has held a sacred status since about 3000 B.C.E. The emperors of China have made a pilgrimage to Tai Shan, in Eastern China, Shandong Province, to be blessed and receive the wisdom to lead their people. Tai Shan is one of five Taoist sacred mountains in China. There are also four Buddhist sacred mountains in China. Muhammad was transfigured on Mount Hira. Mount Vesuvius, the Himalayas, and the Black Hills in South Dakota, all are considered, in some way, the home of the gods (or god).

This story is paired in the lectionary with the Transfiguration stories in the Gospels. As Moses goes up the mountain into the clouds to be with God, so goes Jesus. Both encounter the holy as both prepare to engage the world. They go up to meet with God. They come down to work for God.

Do you ever wonder what sent Moses up there in the first place; to go up to the top of the mountain all by himself to be with God? I recognize that when God gives an invitation, it is hard to say no. It can feel like a scene from the movie *The Godfather* where Don Corleone makes an offer one cannot refuse. But people say no to God all the time. In fact, the Bible can be described as a great narrative of humanity's rebellion and God's redemption. Why did Moses go up the mountain? What did he hear? What was he looking for?

Maybe deep down Moses was afraid; in particular afraid of failure. After coming so far, leading Israel from Egypt to the middle of this wilderness, fear may have swallowed him like a cloud as he wondered would all of this end as a big failure; a miserable experiment of freedom gone awry. He needed answers up that mountain.

Maybe he was lonely. Sure, he has his brother Aaron and sister Miriam nearby, but they are looking to him for answers. They are blaming him when things go wrong. They need him to guide all of them through. It must have been lonely for Moses all those days and nights, listening to people complaining outside his tent and then having to pass along words of God that were not always what they wanted to hear. Up on that mountain was a chance to be alone with God and sort some things out.

Maybe deep within Moses was a longing, a desire, a hope for something more. Even though he had his share of disappointments and setbacks, Moses had lived a good long life. Being a shepherd for your father-in-law is not a bad gig. It was security. Still, there had to be something more and at the ripe old age of 80, Moses was determined to climb that Mountain of God and find out.

Where do you go when you are afraid of failure, or when you are lonely, or when you just want, need, something more in your life? We slave—notice my word choice—we slave away at work and with our families thinking that if we can just work harder, do more things, amass more experiences, try just a little bit more, then we can achieve the pinnacle of self-actualization, self-fulfillment, and self-awareness.

Moses has gotten too old for the kind of naïve foolishness that believes if you just try harder it will all come together. So he goes up the Mountain of God. At first, he is joined by 70 elders. They are the representatives and primary influencers of the institution, the very community of God's people. But they only go so far with Moses. Most of us have experienced when institutions and organizations fall short. Either by choice or decision, they never go all the way up the mountain.

Next, Moses is joined by Joshua. Joshua is the heir apparent, the one who fights for Moses and will succeed Moses when Moses is no more. Joshua represents the next generation. But he too can only go so far. Our legacies, no matter how secure, cannot fully complete us.

In the end, it is just Moses and, as we read in verse 18, Moses disappears into the cloud to be with God on top of the mountain. Whether out of obedience or fear or loneliness or desire, Moses enters the cloud to be with God.

We all—young and old—are looking for something more in life; to be transformed into a larger purpose, a grander vision, a firm standing. Are you willing to risk the Mountain of God? It will change you, because no one can encounter God and remain unchanged.

I am not sure if the anonymous author of "The Cloud of Unknowing" had this text in mind, but I like to think so. The author writes: "All rational beings…possess two faculties, the power of knowing and the power of loving. To the first, to the intellect, God who made them is forever unknowable, but to the second, to love, he is completely knowable."[1]

I am comforted with the thought that intellectually God is unknowable, not that this is an excuse for ignorance—quite the opposite. Science is not to be feared but encouraged, especially as a people of faith. Truth liberates. As we probe deep into the heavens, and peer intently into the genome, I am comforted in knowing that it only reveals deeper mysteries. Quantum physics is as close as you can get to scientific mysticism!

God is unknowable, but still we must climb mountains to know. Moses enters the cloud of unknowing to be enveloped by the glory of God. The Hebrew for glory is "kabod," which can also be translated as abundance. Moses goes with God looking for answers in stone, but something else happens: Moses is enveloped in the abundance of God that transcends speech and knowledge. The Bible says it is for six days before the voice of God is heard, but maybe it is sheer timelessness.

To the intellect God is unknowable. And yet God can be completely and fully known in love. It is the power, the force, the reality that transcends all explanation and knowledge. As I have already asserted in previous messages, the commandments of God are firmly rooted in love. John Killinger wrote a book on the Ten Commandments, the title of which says it all: "To My People With Love."

Moses goes up the mountain to sit awhile with the God who intellectually cannot be fully known and yet through love be completely known. Maybe that is what ultimately sent Moses up the mountain in the first place. Moses needed to know God because Moses loved God's people. Why else would an old man go through all that with Pharaoh and plagues and the relentless complaints of his own people? He loved them and he believed that God must love them too.

God's greatest gesture of love would not be written in stone, but flesh and blood in the person of Jesus. I read an interview about theologian Marcus Borg who said that faithful discipleship is not simply about believing Jesus or believing in a list of beliefs and statements about Jesus. It is to "belove" Jesus. "Faith…is a matter of living in relationship with Jesus…to belove Jesus and walk in his path."[2]

Are you willing to risk the mountain of God? Israel feared it and so did not go. Earlier in Chapter 20, they said to Moses: "You speak to us, and we will listen; but do not let God speak to us, or we will die" (Ex 20:19). Perhaps Moses was afraid too but still he went. What is holding you back from getting face-to-face with God?

What do you do on the Mountain of God? Be still, be quiet, and be ready. Be still. Moses would be up there a long time. Forty days would be the total. In our drive to command all things, be all things, and control all things, being still and doing nothing may be the hardest spiritual discipline of all. We want to do and act and not just sit around to solve our spiritual and psychological impasse.

Be quiet. Only after six days of silence does God give a word. I wonder if for some of us God has difficulty getting a word in because we are busy telling God and anyone else how we are doing. We speak for God in politics, in commerce, in school, and in church, defending our own notions and biasness. Be quiet because God would like to get a word in our loquacious lives.

Be Ready. Things are going to be different for Moses in many ways when he goes down that mountain in forty days—some things for the better and some things will be worse. Moses, however, will be changed. You too, should you risk the Mountain of God, will be changed, so be ready. So that the divine appointment might be complete, what attitude, what area, what habit, what relationship needs to change? Imagine where your church would be if those who went before you were afraid of change?

God is calling you up the mountain; God is calling us all up the mountain. There is a divine appointment and we have been invited. If we want to keep it, there will be a time and season to be still and be quiet that we might be ready, because God will transform us, transform you, and transform the church.

Has God changed you lately? Why not? The mountain waits. We climb mountains to meet God; we descend them to love with God.

MISSIO DEI

[1] Anonymous and A.C. Spearing, *The Cloud of Unknowing and Other Works* (Boston: Penguin Classics, 2002) 63.

[2] John D. Pierce, editor, *Baptists Today,* May 2007.

Missio Dei:
A Meeting Place Along the Way
Exodus 25:1–31:18

A Place to Belong on the Way

Exodus 25:1–28:43

As a preacher, the Sunday after Easter can feel like a real letdown. The crowded sanctuary the week before is emptier, and the enthusiasm has given way to other realities. The days following that first Easter were lonely, too. The disciples were literally dazed and confused about it all and instead of dancing in the streets singing "He is risen," they are locked behind doors convinced they have been abandoned by all, including God. What do you do when God seems to be somewhere else? You set up a meeting place.

For the next three messages, I am going to focus on the teachings of Exodus that are concerned with a meeting place with God. From Chapter 25 through Chapter 31, we will read that a meeting place with God is about a place, a people, and a day—all three are ways we find connection and belonging with God.

Do you have a special place where you like to go and have some time with God, a meeting place? Many years ago, my wife Amy and I built a rather rustic fire pit in the backyard. It is positioned between the lawn and the edge of the woods. No matter what time of year, I can sit on an Adirondack chair and watch the sun set or the stars shine or the blue birds nest and acknowledge with a thankful heart the Holy Creator who made it all. But this is my place. It is not a shared place.

Having a place where we can belong to each other and belong to God is important. As much as we may find these chapters of Exodus as barren ground for post-modern ears—who cares about tabernacle furnishings, and what is a tabernacle anyway?—these chapters address the deep hunger we all have: we need a place to belong and remind us that God is here.

All the major world religions recognize this much. Jews remember the Temple that once stood in Jerusalem, Muslims have the Masjid al-Haram in Mecca, Sikhs crowd into Gurdwara Bangla Sahib Temple in Delhi. Christians have built cathedrals and churches around the world that are a marvel to see.

What if, however, you cannot have a place, because your life is not quite in place, you are on the move and living in transition? That is Israel in this reading. Indeed, that is the history of God's people—never really in one place—pilgrims, wanderers, nomads.

As much as we want to keep things in place, life is never really in place is it? In one form or another, we are always wandering, seeking, looking, and longing. Eric Erikson writes about stages of development. Maslow postulates a hierarchy of needs, progressing from one to the next. Our families are on the move, changing with the times. Our bodies are on the move—the older we get the more things move south! Our faith is even part of this landless sojourn, vacillating between comfort and discomfort.

Throughout Genesis, altars are built along the way, but these are more like mile markers, or those roadside historical signs that indicate something happened here in the past. Israel needed something to remind them that something is happening now along the way.

God gives instruction to Moses (presumably in the clouds, on top of the mountain of God) on the construction of a tabernacle. An offering is taken—an uncomfortable subject for those of us who are particularly sensitive to the accusation that all religious groups want is your money—and the purpose of the offering is to build and furnish a tabernacle.

Tabernacle is first mentioned in Chapter 25 and is referenced no less than 55 times throughout the remainder of Exodus. Something given that much attention in nearly half of Exodus deserves our attention as well, although I dare say the average student of the Bible would not be able to say much about the tabernacle. Additionally, many places in our New Testament assume an understanding of the Old Testament as it makes comparisons. You need to know about the Tabernacle in order to make sense of the book of Hebrews, particularly Chapters 8 and 9. Paul the apostle makes references in the book of Romans. Likewise, the Book of Revelation is filled with references of the Tabernacle and its furnishings.

What then is the Tabernacle? It literally means a "dwelling place," as in a tent. It is also called in Exodus a "Tent of Meeting" and occasionally it is called a sanctuary. The tabernacle housed the ark of the covenant, an incense altar, a table, a seven-light candelabra called a "menorah," Aaron's staff that miraculously budded (Numbers 17:23ff), the vessels that are used by the priests, a container of manna, and a scroll written by Moses. The Tabernacle was a literal place where the people of God could belong. They could say, "I go there." The place, like the people, was designed to be on the move, a sanctuary on wheels.

It is not that God *has* to have a place. In the Bible, God is experienced in all kinds of random places from burning bushes to voices in the clouds. The sacred space of the Tabernacle points to two essential realities: 1) God goes with you 2) You go with God.

God Goes with You

God goes with you, so God is with you. Verse 8 tells us the purpose of this tabernacle for Israel: "…so that I may dwell with them" (Ex 25:8). There is no question that Israel, newly freed and completely landless, needed this reminder. You are not in Egypt; you are wandering all over this vast wilderness of a desert; the land you dream of is still far away and a long way off. Wherever you are, God goes with you.

We need tabernacles to remind us in our landless, wandering places that God joins with us in our life's sojourn; our transitions.

The tabernacle is a tent and so with a little effort it could be moved literally anywhere. Worship was not a fixed or exclusive place. As important as Mt. Sinai is—it is called, after all, the Mountain of God—it is not holy. Only God is holy and God's presence is what makes a place holy. God goes with you.

It reminds me of part of the Prayer of St. Patrick:

"Christ with me, Christ before me, Christ behind me,
Christ in me, Christ beneath me, Christ above me,
Christ on my right, Christ on my left,
Christ when I lie down, Christ when I sit down,
Christ in the heart of everyone who thinks of me,
Christ in the mouth of everyone who speaks of me,
Christ in the eye that sees me,
Christ in the ear that hears me."[1]

How does God go with you? In Exodus 25:2, there is this wonderful line requesting an offering for the Tabernacle: "all whose hearts prompt them." This is not mandatory and neither is it a tax. The Hebrew expression is literally "all whose hearts make them willing."[2] God goes with you when you make room in your heart for God.

Compare this to the hard heart of Pharaoh, who had no room for God or God's promises. The liberated heart of the Israelites was open to new realities and possibilities. The tabernacle becomes the external symbol of an internal reality. I love the earthiness of the tabernacle. It was a reminder that God has not abandoned creation to live in the heavens, but that God is right here on the earth with the people. The Sages of the Mishnah calculate that the tabernacle was built on Yom Kippur, the Day of Atonement, as a reminder that no matter how far we have strayed, God chooses to pitch a tent with us as we wander along.

The tabernacle reminds us that God *goes with you*. It is also a reminder, a commission, that:

You Go with God

A tabernacle, nor any other house, or tent or temple can contain, confine, or otherwise keep God in God's place. In Kings 8:27, Solomon says, "But will God indeed dwell on the earth? Even heaven and the highest heaven cannot contain you, much less this house that I have built!"

Tabernacles are just like anything else we build with our hands—temporary. One day all our earthly structures will be no more. This story is not just that God goes with us, but that we are called to go with God into a world needing to be touched by grace, love, and redemption.

Easter is called a moveable feast because it falls on different dates on the calendar. It is not fixed. It is appropriate that on a Sunday after Easter we read a text that reminds us God will not be put "in place" either and neither should we. Our loftiest ideas, our crafted theologies, the oldest traditions, and our most novel innovations will not and cannot contain God. We go with God.

In the Gospel of John, the writer had this passage in mind when he wrote: "The Word became flesh and dwelt among us" (Jn 1:14). In the original Greek, it is translated "tabernacle" or more simply, "pitched his tent" with us. What a lovely thought. What a lovely idea. What a lovely gift. Later in this same Gospel, Jesus prays, "I in them and you in me, that they may become completely one, so that the world may know that you have sent me and have loved them even as you have loved me" (Jn 17:23). Jesus "tabernacled" among us and has now gone ahead.

God pitches his tent with us, right here among us, and we too are called up into the holy sojourn to go with God in this trek through life. You see we do not just find God when we go to church. We find that when we leave church, God has already left the building inviting us into the world.

God goes with you now. Go with God. Vaya con Dios…God with ye… buen camino…dominus vobiscum…Go with God for God goes with you.

Go with God as you prepare for the routines of work this week.

Go with God in the classroom.
Go with God into a world that is thirsty for peace.
Go with God.

[1] "The Prayer of St. Patrick," *beliefnet*, https://www.beliefnet.com/prayers/catholic/morning/the-prayer-of-st-patrick.aspx.

[2] J. Gerald Janzen, *Exodus* (Louisville: Westminster John Knox Press, 1997) 193.

A People to Belong with on the Way

Exodus 29:1–31:11

In the previous message, the text was concerned with a meeting place for God, so the tabernacle was constructed. Wherever Israel would go, the tabernacle would go as a sign of the presence of God. On the way, God goes with Israel and on the way, Israel goes with God.

This text is also concerned with a meeting place manifested through people; specifically, priests. Priests provided, through ritual and service, the idea of belonging to God. Not just anyone could be a priest. Only Aaron and his decedents could serve as priests.

This whole chapter is grisly with the details of ordination, which included the ritual slaughter and butchering of animals. At one point, in the middle of Chapter 29, we read that the fat of a ram, the fat from the tail, the fat that covers the entrails, the appendage of the liver, two kidneys, the right thigh, a loaf of bread and a cake of bread were to be placed in the hands of Aaron and his sons as part of the ordination service. How would you like to go to an ordination service like that? As an aside, the Hebrew word for "ordain" means "to be full." All I got for my ordination was a Bible.

According to another book in the Torah, Leviticus, Israel's priests served as:

1. Military chaplains accompanying the armies into battle
2. Doctors (less for treatment and more for diagnosis)
3. Mediators between the people and YHWH
4. Butchers regarding the sacrifice of animals including bulls, rams, goats, and sheep.

The priest's essential role was that of a mediator, a go-between the people and God. As mediator, the priest shares with the prophet. The priest intercedes on their behalf through ritual; the prophet intercedes through proclamation and prayers. The welfare of Israel depends on both Moses the prophet and Aaron the priest.

Today, Jews no longer sacrifice animals or grains on an altar. This formally ended with the destruction of the Temple in 70 AD. Some years back, I asked one of my rabbi friends how Jews honor the intention of sacrifice in modern times. He reminded me that three times a day Jews are to pray the "Amidah," which in its origins was a prayer of 19 "benedictions." After the Temple's destruction, the Council of Jamnia determined that the Amidah would substitute for the sacrifices, a practice still in place two thousand years later.

Earlier in Exodus, we read of Israel, "you shall be for me a priestly kingdom and a holy nation" (Ex 19:6). As Christians, we understand Jesus as the "High Priest." In Hebrews Chapter 4, it is written: "Since, then, we have a great high priest who has passed through the heavens, Jesus, the Son of God, let us hold fast to our confession. For we do not have a high priest who is unable to sympathize with our weaknesses, but we have one who in every respect has been tested as we are, yet without sin" (Ex 4: 14–15).

As our priest, Jesus makes the sacrifice, indeed is the sacrifice, and is the perfect mediator between God and us.

First Peter 2:5, 9 says, "…like living stones, let yourselves be built into a spiritual house, to be a holy priesthood…but you are a chosen race, a royal priesthood, a holy nation, God's own people."

At the risk of trivializing the text, the New Testament writer is inviting us to don a clerical collar as we are called—each of us, all of us—to the priesthood. Through Christ, we are a royal priesthood, a holy priesthood, a kingdom or realm of priests. Sounds pretty impressive, doesn't it? The priesthood of all believers is a central tenet in Protestantism since the 16th century and a uniting idea in Baptist thought. Baptist historian Walter Shurden writes that the priesthood of all or every believer is "the freedom and responsibility of every person to relate directly to God without imposition of creed or control of clergy or government."[1]

What does "priesthood of all believers" mean to us today? Has God bestowed upon us an honor and a privilege and today God meets us here to bask in our own radiance? No. Brothers and sisters, God meets us here because soul freedom calls for responsibility—God has something for those of us in the priesthood to do.

There are a few things that this soul freedom is not. It is not extreme individualism, for we are baptized into communion. It never exists unto itself. That is, soul freedom is balanced among the other freedoms. Finally, it is not limited to Baptists.

Here are four implications to this ancient text for today's people:

1. You are qualified.

The Gospels tell of a time when Jesus was walking among his disciples and posed a question to them, "Who do people say that the Son of Man is?" (Mt 16:13). It was a personal question that demanded a personal response. The disciples' reaction was fairly typical and even predictable. They began to blurt out what all the experts were saying—here is the prophet's opinion; here is what the crowds are saying. If he were to ask that question of us today, we might respond, "Here is what the seminaries are saying, here is what the Cooperative Baptist Fellowship says, here is the latest resolution from the Southern Baptist Convention, or this is what Greg has said in one of his sermons."

But the question is a personal one. Jesus leveled his question directly to the disciples and to us, "But who do you say that I am?" Part of our Baptist identity is affirming that each of us has an individual responsibility concerning our faith. Soul freedom means that individually we are competent in matters of faith—with or without a seminary degree!

Walter Shurden notes, "Some people, it seems, will do almost anything to avoid the responsibility for their lives." C. Brownlow Hastings writes: "…the final choice of belief and practice must be made in the secret of the soul's naked presence before God alone."[2]

Soul freedom means the right to choose, and also the right to reject: "Choose this day whom you will serve…" (Josh 24:15). It is our choice to choose or reject Christ, not someone else's. In the end, when we face God, what will count is not what others think—Baptists, Catholics, Presbyterians, clergy, mom and dad, etc. What will matter is how we each answer the personal question: "Who do you say that I am?"

2. You are experienced.

In other words, one's relationship with God is not just about experiencing God in community, but it is also a personal one. Your parents cannot do it for you, ones' church cannot do it for you—it is your experience. Sometimes our experiences take on a dramatic tone (road to Damascus), but sometimes it is far more subtle (never knowing a time when Christ was not part of one's life). But it is to be your own experience and not someone else's.

My first "experience" was reciting the Lord's Prayer as a child and staring at a portrait of Jesus behind the pulpit in my daddy's church. The next came while watching a Billy Graham crusade on TV. I subsequently gave my life over to Christ's keeping. But my experiences did not stop there. Another came subtly one morning when I awoke to go to the barn for milking and knew that God was calling me into full time service to the church. There was the time, a few years later, that Unity Baptist Church took a chance and called a 21-year-old to serve as their pastor.

Soul freedom is acknowledging an experience with the living Jesus. One time, a man who was blind since birth was questioned by the religious authorities as to who healed him from his blindness. The man did not know all of the doctrines or teachings of scripture; he did not know what the institutions would think or the opinions of the synagogue. The man who was healed did not even have time to counsel with his preacher. He simply said, "One thing I do know, that though I was blind, now I see" (Jn 9:25).

Soul freedom means that everyone who calls themselves a Christian should have an ongoing personal experience with the living Jesus.

3. You are ordained.

That is, God has filled your hands with the work you need to do. Remember Moses and his hand holding to his staff way back in Exodus 4? Bill Leonard writes, "All Christians are called to be priests, ministering to one another and sharing the love of God to the world."[3] We are *all* called, not a select, reserved, or otherwise special number.

There are many times I find myself wanting a symbol for my office as a "professional minister"—you know, something like a clerical collar. A priest can waltz into a hospital and instantly be recognized as an ordained official of the church, in whom lies all sorts of spiritual secrets and ecclesiastical goodies. I come into a hospital and people assume I work with food services or maybe a grounds keeper who just likes to wear a tie. There are some who think I look ministerial. In one of my former pastorates, the local funeral home staff was convinced that if I would just wear a yarmulke I could pass as a Jewish rabbi.

Truth is, as a Baptist, the only symbol for my office is me. I am a priest not because of the kind of clothes I wear, not because I went to seminary, and not because I can put "Reverend" in front of my name. In fact, Baptists believe that every believer serves a priestly role and function.

The great Baptist preacher/theologian Carlyle Marney once wrote that we Baptists often interpret the priesthood of all believers as advocating that we do not need priests. But he reminds us that yes, we do! "We need people who will listen to us with God's ears and speak God's word to us."⁴ The idea is not to get rid of priests but to spread the responsibility around. "But you are a chosen race, a royal priesthood, a holy nation, God's own people, in order that you may proclaim the mighty acts of him who called you out of darkness into his marvelous light" (1 Pet 2:9).

So who are the priests among us? Preachers—yes, they serve this role. But so do deacons, the missionary groups who meet each month, nursery workers, sound technicians, custodians, and the quiet person on the pew—come to think of it—everyone who calls on Christ as their Lord and Savior serves a priestly role. And you do not even need to wear a clerical collar!

4. You are responsible.

Dr. Tim Owings, former pastor of First Baptist Church of Augusta, preached a sermon many years ago about soul freedom, or competency, as he described it. He said that for Baptists, soul competency meant a privilege, ability, and a responsibility. That pretty much sums up this final point. We have been set apart, ordained, to be priests to others. Yes, the clerical collar fits you too.

In Acts, we read of a day when John and Peter were going up to the temple to pray. There they were "accosted" by a beggar asking for money. "But Peter said, 'I have no silver or gold, but what I have I give you; in the name of Jesus Christ of Nazareth, stand up and walk'" (Acts 3:6). Soul freedom is giving to others what you have in Christ.

Again, we hear from the great Baptist historian Walter Shurden: "Priests have two purposes: they bring God to people, and they bring people to God." John Hewett writes, "The task of priests is to connect the heart of God with the hearts of people in ways faithful to both."⁵

We are to take their priestly role with seriousness. We have to look deeply into the needs around us, as close as our own elbow. And looking is the very thing our society discourages. A couple of weeks ago, I was in Washington, D.C., and while walking between the hotel and the conference center I found myself going into "urban mode" and refused to make eye contact with people. Keep walking, don't look. Be careful with whom you share a smile—they may want something from me after all.

But we—you and I—are called to be God's priests here on earth. And if we are going to be faithful to our priestly calling then we have little choice but to look: look at the empty hands begging for a bit of change; look into the eyes of the elderly man stricken with loneliness; look at the sticky cheeks of a child who needs desperately to hear they are special. Just look—and do not call out for the minister or some specialist to solve the problem. You, too, are God's own priest.

[1] Walter Shurden, *The Baptist Identity: Four Fragile Freedoms* (Macon GA: Smyth & Helwys Publishing, 1993) 1.

[2] Ibid., 31.

[3] Cecil P. Staton Jr., editor, *Why I Am a Baptist: Reflections on Being Baptist in the 21st Century* (Macon GA: Smyth & Helwys Publishing, 1999) 85.

[4] Walter B. Shurden, *Proclaiming the Baptist Vision: The Priesthood of all Believers* (Macon, GA: Smyth & Helwys Publishing, 1993) 68.

[5] Ibid., 63.

A Day to Belong on the Way

Exodus 31:12–18

Two words: Jimmy Buffett. Even if you are not a fan, chances are you have heard of him. He is known and celebrated as a man who loves to sing about doing nothing: a license to chill, sleeping in the hammock, escaping to an island. He is one of the most popular musicians in our time with sold-out concerts in every city he tours. I went to one of those a few years ago and was amused to see that he draws from nearly every age group. He sings about what most of us fantasize about: the joy of doing nothing!

I should point out to you that God said it first! These last few sermons we have been exploring meeting places with God. The tabernacle, the tent of meeting, was holiness of space. The priesthood was the holiness of people and, through the fulfillment of Jesus, we are all priests, holy to God. Today, we examine meeting God through the holiness of time—keeping the Sabbath. A place, a people, and now a time are ways we have a meeting with God.

Remember when Sunday meant something? Well those days are gone for nearly all of us. Now Sunday—the Sabbath for most Christians—looks like most any other day of the week. It is hard to find a store of any kind that is closed on Sunday. We give polite lip service to those few businesses that out of conviction are not open on Sunday, but the truth is it would be more convenient to us if they would just open up because we want to eat or shop. Recreation leagues have games and practices year round for their sports, many of them scheduled at the same time as Sunday worship. Of course, since the founding of our country, other religions have accommodated around the Christian calendar, but now we are all competing with the same seven-day per week schedule where literally nothing is sacred, not even our days.

I guess I should warn you up front this will be no ordinary "keep the Sabbath" sermon. Before I go there, let me point out a few highlights. The first time we read about Sabbath in the Bible is in Exodus Chapter 16. Prior to Israel's liberation, there is no command, per se, regarding the Sabbath. It is true that in Genesis 2 we read that God blessed the seventh day and rested, but there is no commandment given at this point. Yet the Sabbath, or the seventh day, was the first thing that God sanctified. Before there were laws or covenants, rules or rituals, there was the blessing making sacred space of time. Furthermore, the seventh day on our calendars is not Sunday, because that is the first day of the week. The seventh day is Saturday. Jews observe the Sabbath starting at sundown on Friday and ending at sundown on Saturday. The early Christians did the same but by the eighth century, Sunday was considered the Christian Sabbath because this was the day of Jesus' resurrection, hence the phrase, "the Lord's Day."

In Exodus, we read now that the treasured people of God have been set free. They are told, indeed they are commanded, to take a break.

We tend to read this text and get understandably distracted and upset with the line, "Whoever does any work on the Sabbath shall be put to death." Is it just me, or don't you think that seems rather extreme? Was this a hyperbole or is God serious about this? Israel took it seriously. There is a story in the book of Numbers of a man gathering sticks on the Sabbath. He is subsequently apprehended, taken out of the encampment, and stoned to death. There is not much I can say to defend or even explain this away other than to point out that for the ancients this was a sign of rebellion within the ranks. Rebellion cannot be tolerated when you are trying to keep it together through a harsh wilderness on the way to a better life.

It is easy to forget the larger story. We forget that in Egypt there was no rest. We forget that when the people of Israel were simply called Hebrews, which was its own form of a slave name, there was no day off because human dignity meant nothing to the dominant power of Pharaoh. This is the guy, after all, who tossed baby boys in the Nile to be destroyed. Life meant nothing to him and therefore Israel's time meant nothing.

Sabbath was a means to speak truth to power. To neglect it is deadly. Pharaoh wants you to believe you are only as valuable as your work, your labor, your usefulness. Oh, and by the way, you can never, ever work enough to catch up.

God said you and I are created for more than someone else's exploitation. You and I are valued for more than the quota of bricks we make and the pyramids we build. To not observe a Sabbath is to assert that you are better than God. "It is a sign forever between me and the people of Israel that in six days the LORD made heaven and earth, and on the seventh day he rested, and was refreshed" (Ex 31:17). God took a break; so can you.

We are told that it is a sign twice in the text. That is how God's people are to be identified in the world of Egypt and Pharaohs. It is a sign that you are worth more to God than your productivity. It is common in religious devotion to think we must do something for God. Here, God is saying that if you want to belong to me, *do nothing*!

To believe in our work to the expense of ourselves and others is to effectively disbelieve God and to exchange our covenant with God back to Pharaoh. I think that is exactly what many are doing in this world today. We no longer believe in God, according to our work, and Pharaoh has returned to rule our lives. If you do not believe me, show me your schedule, and I will show you your devotion.

So what do we do? We have a commandment given to us for the third time in the book of Exodus and our excuses on why we do not keep a Sabbath are not defensible; unless of course you do not believe any of this, unless of course you would rather work for Pharaoh than rest with God.

So what do we do? Well, I am not advocating that we return to a time in which laws restrict businesses on when they can open and what they can sell. That is in the end silliness. Neither am I suggesting we boycott places because of their choices on when to open and what to do.

We have to declare a Sabbath and keep it. To do this, we need a better definition of what we mean by Sabbath and when we observe it. As I look over both the Old and New Testaments regarding the Sabbath and how it was observed, abused, and, particularly during the time of Jesus, misunderstood, there are three simple ways our Jewish friends remind us of what keeping Sabbath is: the Sabbath is a day of holiness, rest, and joy. John Killinger simplifies this as the "Three R's": remembering, resting, and rejoicing.[1]

Holiness (Remembering)

"Remember the Sabbath and keep it holy." That is how the fourth commandment is given in Exodus 20:8. For Jews, it is the most holy day of the year and it comes every week. Holy means in part that it is "set aside" for God. In the context of Exodus, it is a subversive act to the week dominated by Pharaoh and survival and entering into the trust of God's provision. It is a holy act to remember the Sabbath.

How can we make our Sabbath holy? Worship is, of course, one way, and an important one at that. We use this day to remember that it was on the Lord's Day that the women came to the tomb and found it empty. We remember that in a world that seeks to redefine our value, God loves us unconditionally. We remember that we are created for a purpose other than the sins that so often stain our speech and action. We remember that we are to seek out reconciliation with others, forgiving as we are forgiven. We do this by singing together, learning together, proclaiming together. We do this by hearing the old stories and being inspired by the new stories.

We keep the Sabbath holy by remembering who God is and who we are as created in the image of God. That gives us strength for the rest of the week.

Rest

God rested and was refreshed. Yes, I realize how anthropocentric this all sounds, but the idea is worth reflection. The root of Sabbath means, "to catch one's breath." There is a marvelous Hebrew word that gives us a picture of Sabbath rest: *vayinafosh*. It means simply, "God took a breath."

Any of you need a break? Do you really need me to point out how overscheduled our lives are and how we are dragging our children down with us in our state of perpetual fatigue? We have even made our playtime feel more like work. Our bodies, minds, and spirits are worn out and Sunday is just one more day in a full, full week.

In writing this sermon, I recognized how ironic it was because I also had to prepare and preach a different sermon for this past Friday; attend a conference and serve as a facilitator for a break-out session on Saturday, today I will have a premarital counseling session, a funeral, an evening worship, but before all of that I have to preach this sermon on taking a rest! I doubt I am exceptional in regard to my schedule.

Once I went around asking some of my staff and fellow ministers if they carved out time on a weekly basis for rest. Most of us struggle with having true downtime. Some talked about sleeping late on Saturdays. One said that she does not check her email on her day off and uses that same day to play with the children and read books. Another minister extolled the value of finding some time on Sunday to take a nap. I have a friend of mine who is a pastor who takes Monday off and that is her day of Sabbath rest. One of the things she does is unplugs completely—no email! We are burdened with the schedules and habits seven days a week.

You and I are created and valued for more than just our productivity. Find time this week and each week and declare it as a Sabbath rest.

Joy (Rejoicing)

Over the years, I have heard and preached my fair share of sermons on keeping the Sabbath. It is one of those commandments we know we "ought to do" but for the most part ignore. Why is this? Maybe some of us older ones remember growing up in a time when keeping the Sabbath was a strict, joyless day: just church, Bible reading, and maybe visiting with family, but no fishing, swimming, and certainly no going to the movies. Here in the South, there were laws that made sure there would be little joy on the Sabbath because everything was closed. I suppose I am being too harsh because there is little joy in working all the time or because of our own consumption habits having others work all the time.

What is it that gives you joy? Declare it as such and thank God for it. Sitting outdoors, running with your dogs, planting flowers, or watching honeybees. Someone mentioned to me of a rabbi reflecting that Sabbath was creating space and time for happiness to catch up to you.

We typically ask people we meet, "So what do you do for a living?" What we want to know is what is that person's work or occupation. Maybe a better question is not "What do you do for a living?" but "What do you do for play?" A member asked me what I would be preaching on as I was preparing this message. When I said it would be on the importance of keeping the Sabbath, he quickly added: "I hope it is okay to play golf." Only if it is play and not work!

It has long been convenient to criticize the younger generation for failing to appreciate the value of hard work. But I wonder if we are valuing the joy of Sabbath—the "un-work" spaces in life? Sometimes I think we have made "play" to be just more work.

Sabbath in its Old Testament usage was often connected with feasting. Nehemiah 8: 9–10 says, "This day is holy to the Lord your God; do not mourn or weep….Go your way, eat the fat and drink sweet wine and send portions to him for whom nothing is prepared; for this day is holy to our Lord; and do not be grieved, for the joy of the Lord is your strength."

I wear a self-winding watch, so when it is not worn on my wrist it will eventually stop. I was amused when I glanced at my watch on the nightstand after I had returned from a week of vacation and discovered it stopped keeping time on the day I left.

We all need spaces and places where we are not ruled by our schedules or defined by our productivity. Is it any wonder that when God completed six days of work, God declared a Sabbath for the seventh? I hope that in the course of your week, you find the time to take your watch off, rest, and know that your value is not in what you do, but who you are—a child of God.

[1] John Killinger, *To My People With Love: The Ten Commandments for Today*, (Nashville: Abingdon Press, 1988), 55.

Missio Dei:
In Failure and Restoration
Exodus 32:1–34:35

Lose Your Religion

Exodus 32:1–35

The children of God called Israel—a name rooted in striving—has been claimed by God, freed by God, and now invited into a covenant, a relationship, with God. Yet failure is just a decision away. For the next few sermons we will examine and see what failure looks like and what restoration looks like for all those called and claimed of God.

This is a salacious story. Not so long ago, we read with a hint of mysticism of Moses entering into the cloud on top of Mt. Sinai to be alone with God. On this Mountain of God, Moses will hear the voice of God and receive instructions, which include the Ten Commandments on tablets of stone, written, we read, by the finger of God. Moses has led the people thus far out of duty and command and the people have depended on Moses. But now, he is on top of a mountain and left them alone for a few days that became a week, and still more weeks pass with no Moses. He is gone for forty days and nights before coming down that mountain with the two tablets in hand and a fresh vision of where they need to go.

What a good feeling that must be for Moses: having a mountain top experience with God and heading back to re-engage the world with a vision and a plan of action. It is like going on a retreat or a vacation. You are re-charged and refreshed and return with a sense of revitalized purpose.

What Moses did not know, could not know, was that while he was having his holy moment with the Holy Other, the people were rife with anxiety that they were now all alone in this wilderness. No Moses and no home and it even felt like there was no God either. Have you ever dwelt in the tabernacle of loneliness, as if you were abandoned by all, even God? That was Israel.

There is no question that religion can lose its luster when the wilderness goes deep and our securities get threatened. When religion isn't relevant, it leads to crisis. It is a breakdown of faith where the old is no longer working or does not work in the same way. We all have or we will have encounters that shake our faith to its very core.

Let me tell you about an elderly lady who for decades struggled against the silence and seeming absence of God—a religious crisis like none other. Few knew of her struggles; they only saw this great woman of faith and service. Following her death, some of her letters were published. In one she wrote: "The silence and emptiness is great where I look and do not see, listen but do not hear." We may envision such a lady as just another weak-willed apostate, fickle in the faith and focused on worldly things instead of heavenly bliss. This was no frail failure. She was the revered—some call saint—Mother Teresa. She once told a friend, "Jesus has a very special love for you. [But] as for me—The silence and the emptiness is so great—that I look and do not see,—Listen and do not hear."[1]

I do not think there is anything wrong with a crisis of faith, spiritual anxiety, or a religious meltdown (or whatever you want to call it). As I said, I believe it happens to all of us. It was happening to Israel. It is a matter of where you will go when the wilderness gets thick and the way out no longer seems easy or obvious or clearly mapped. There in the wilderness, Israel is at a crossroads.

Israel chose a god they could not in the end digest. In their fear and anxiety, they begged of Aaron, the brother of Moses and spokesperson to the people, to fashion some gold-plated reassurance in the form of a calf. They needed something, some substitute, because it seemed their best access to God was gone. "Come, make gods for us, who shall go before us; as for this Moses, the man who brought us up out of the land of Egypt, we do not know what has become of him" (Ex 32:1). The golden calf became the material symbol of their sin. In fact, it may not be too much of a stretch to say that all sin, stripped to its very essence is embodied in this story of failure.

The people's problem was not that they lost their religion. Indeed, they were deeply religious. They were, however, willing to settle for anything; willing to settle for any substitute that would fill the void. It is my belief that we rush too quickly to fill our empty places in life with things, beliefs, ideologies, when maybe God would have us to linger a while in the absence; in the liminal places and listen to the stillness. We are afraid to be still and quiet and choose gods of noise and distraction and empty entertainment.

When Moses comes down the mountain, it is not pretty. Joshua thinks all the shouting is a gathering for war but Moses knows: the kids have thrown a party while the parent is out of town. It is revelry. Moses dashes the tablets at the foot of the mountain, breaking them to pieces and then he does something rather odd. Moses "…took the calf that they had made, burned it with fire ground it to powder, scattered it on the water, and made the Israelites drink it" (Ex 32:20).

Was this punishment? Was this intended to be a lesson such as the saying: "you made your bed, now sleep in it"? Everything seems to be coming apart at the foot of the Mountain of God. The people have fallen apart. The tablets of stone of the covenant are broken to pieces. Moses is mad and God's wrath is smoldering and now the calf has been ground into golden Kool-Aid and they are told to drink it up.

The people called the "treasured possession" of God are at a crossroads. At the crossroads in the wilderness Israel was confronted with three basic questions that confront us all at the important junctures of life: Who am I? Where am I going? How will I get there?

This story is concerned primarily with the question of how; how will I get there? Indeed, that is one of the essential functions of religion—identity, purpose, and principle. In answering the question of "how," Israel chose the route of convenient substitutes and quick fixes. They chose a god that could be domesticated and manipulated for their own purposes and destiny.

If the religion you follow is nothing more than a thin veneer of easy substitutes and quick fixes, then it is best to lose your religion, at least that one. Likewise, if how you get through in life is by depending on a religion that has domesticated God in a manipulated image—lose it.

Be careful, for the temptation is great that you will want to substitute your religion for another. I once heard Bill Leonard preach a sermon on this text, and he asked the question, "What gods are you drinking?"[2] We have the usual list of "isms"—nationalism, materialism, consumerisms. Out of fear, we want a god that will assure us security. Out of envy, we want a god that will produce for us goods and services.

What are your golden calves; your divine substitutes? Maybe it is a church building, especially when it is no longer seen as a resource for God's mission, but an institution. Could the Bible be a divine substitute? People argue over the Bible as if it was the Bible that saves a soul instead of Jesus. Maybe it is a partisan political cause you are convinced will save this troubled nation. Let's not delude ourselves—we have our golden calves. And like Israel, it is not because we have lost our religion; we are just willing to make substitutes.

Too often we have substituted a *relationship* with God with *religion* and have created for ourselves golden calves of the "right" way of doing things, observing empty rituals and upholding the high maintenance of institutional faith. Well it is time to lose it. It is time to tear down the golden calves we have fashioned out of our anxiety, out of our loneliness, out of our emptiness, out of our anger. Lose that religion of indigestible gods and drink deeply what God has to offer.

To the violence and poverty and desperation of our times, bow down to the One who said you are all created in the Image of God. Our intrinsic worth as human beings is given by God and therefore cannot be imaged in fixed preoccupations of golden calves or anything else made by our hands or minds.

The only image acceptable for God is the one we wake up to each day. You want a glimpse of God? Look in the mirror; look to your neighbor; glance to the custodian pushing a broom and to the nursery worker changing a diaper; consider even your enemy and there you will see image-bearers of the Holy. No one image is whole or complete or definitive.

You and I are God's handiwork and we "…are fearfully and wonderfully made" (Ps 139:14). In Psalm 8, we hear the prayer, "…what are human beings that you are mindful of them, mortals that you care for them? Yet you have made them a little lower than God, and crowned them with glory and honor" (Ps 8:4–5).

The incarnation reminds us that God really does want to be with us… all of us, so there can never ever be any substitutes. Christ in you is what you need most to face your future and to confront this generation's challenges. Not your talents or gifts or lack of. Not substitutions and quick fixes. You in Christ and Christ in you.

To the questions of "who" and "where," I cannot answer for you. And you will answer those questions differently along the way. But to question of "how," my answer is simple for those in the Christian community: go with Christ.

Israel thought they could have a tangible god subject to personal use, a predictable god that could be controlled when necessary, a convenient god, free from discipline. The great sin was substituting El-Shaddai, God Almighty, for a domesticated god that is both manageable and expedient. That is when religion is misplaced, and like the golden calf, it is best to get rid of it.

We destroy the golden calves of false religion by remembering that the future is not in our hands, which is what Israel sought to wrangle over at the foot of the holy mountain. The future has always been with the Lord of history and time, and what does the Bible say about this future? "Surely there is a future, and your hope will not be cut off" (Prov. 23:18).

In the image of God we are blessed and purposed.

In the image of God we birth babies and dignify holy callings.

In the image of God we are charged to create and care.

Go ahead, lose your religion based on the golden calf of quick fixes, immediate replies, simplistic solutions and overnight success, and commit yourself to the long, obedient journey.

The prophet Isaiah writes:

> "But those who wait for the LORD
> shall renew their strength,
> they shall mount up with wings like eagles,
> they shall run and not be weary,
> they shall walk and not faint" (Isa 40:31).

Who will join me in losing one's religion? That there will be no substitutes for God, even things as attractive as religion; that we will wait on God and not settle for quick fixes of faith; that control belongs to God, and not the other way around; and resolving to accept that the mercy of God is extended to all of us who lose the way and serve golden calves.

[1] David Van Biema, "Mother Teresa's Crisis of Faith," *Time*, August 23, 2007, https://time.com/4126238/mother-teresas-crisis-of-faith/.

Facing Glory...and Surviving

Exodus 33:1–23

Sometimes the most important thing we can do is to simply show up. It doesn't matter if you are not the most successful member in your family, but show up at the reunion. It doesn't matter if you are working long hours to provide the very best for your children, but show up at the dinner table. It doesn't matter if you do not know what to say to your friend whose spouse died, but show up to share a hug. Sometimes the most important thing we can do is to simply show up. In our story today Moses wants God to show up.

The most common prayer we hear in church is "Lord, be in this place," that is, show up. But isn't God everywhere? Where else would God be if not right here, in this place? We pray for God's presence, not just in church, but in pivotal events in life. "Lord, be present to me as I go through this illness… this marriage…this trial with my children…this hardship…Lord, be present to these parents, these babies…Lord, be present, show up." Maybe we pray for God to be present because we know what absence feels like. We know what it feels like to be all alone. We need assurances and reassurances that God is there, that God is here.

In our story today, God is threatening to not show up. God is having, in my loose translation of the original Hebrew, a hissy fit with Israel. They made a golden calf as a tangible substitute for the "Real Deal." Now the idol is ground up into a powdered drink mix and the tablets of the Ten Commandments are smashed to pieces. God says to Moses something no one wants to hear: "Go up to a land flowing with milk and honey, but I will not go up among you" (Ex 33:3).

Whoa. Have you ever crossed a line with someone you love and because of it the entire relationship changed? I have worked with couples where one or both have been unfaithful and, although many times the marriage survives, it is never the same again. This is what seems to be happening here. At least how this story is told, it reads like God is ready to give up on them. Can God do that? In fact, in the previous chapter, right after the debacle of the golden calf, the language reads that Israel is disavowed and disowned. God says to Moses: "*Your* people, whom *you* brought up out of the land of Egypt have acted perversely" (Ex 32:7, emphasis added). Notice how God no longer calls Israel "my people." Instead, he tells Moses, "you take them." It is like parents going through a divorce and one says to the other, you take custody of the kids. I can't handle them. Go on to the land promised to you, but I am not going with you. The Lord is *not* in this place.

Moses goes and makes a case for Israel. He slips into the Tent of Meeting, the Tabernacle we have been hearing so much about, and he appeals for God to show up. I like Moses. He is a spunky old man, especially when it comes to taking on God. For a guy with a speech problem, he has little problem talking to God. He argues with God. He negotiates with God. He pleads with God. He begs of God. He does not give up on God. In other words, Moses knows how to pray. Most of us pray those deferential kinds of prayers that sound like we really don't believe God is going to do anything but will ask anyway for the sake of ceremony and appearance. No, the prayer of Moses is a prayer that takes God serious enough to believe that God might respond.

Moses says to God: "Show me your ways" (Ex 33.13). That is another way of asking for God to show up. Plenty of times throughout life we will feel as though God has left the building and left our lives for good. Lord, give me a sign that you are up there, that you are listening, that you care. "Show me your ways," is the demand of Moses, and those words can be our words when we fear God has abandoned us. In fear it is tempting to substitute God with cheap imitations.

Moses prays, "I am not giving up on you God and I don't want you giving up on us." I really do not think God is disowning or giving up, but I do understand this story as telling us how serious the offense is to God. Because the offense is so serious, the people certainly would have wondered how their relationship with God could ever be restored after what they had done. Have you ever crossed that line with God where you feel as though God has just given up and checked out on you? You need reassurance of God's presence.

"Show me your ways." How does that look today, to see the ways of God? We read the Bible to understand the ways of God through the ancient lives of others. We worship and fellowship to share our stories and celebrate the ways of God in them. Most of us would rather see a sermon, after all, than hear one. How do you see the ways of God in our world?

Moses doesn't just stop there. He then says to God: "Show me your glory" (Ex 33:18). Rabbis teach that glory is one of the most important words in biblical theology. In the Hebrew, it is *kabod* and in addition to "glory," it can be translated as "abundance" or "honor." The visual image found elsewhere in the scripture is something like an overwhelming or overpowering light.

"Show me your glory" was Moses' way of saying, "Let me see everything, God." The big picture. The answer is somewhat deflected by God saying in the next verse, "I will let you see my goodness; I will let you know my name; you will see my graciousness and my mercy" (Ex 33:19).

Okay, we are getting somewhere. God *is* going to show up in Israel's wanderings through goodness, and name, and through grace and mercy. God has not left them after all. Moses wants more. As I mentioned earlier, this guy knows how to talk to God. "Show me your glory—I am serious."

In the ensuing dialogue, God says something to the effect, "You cannot handle all of me." And so Moses plays a celestial version of peek-a-boo with God. God takes a hand, hides Moses' face, slips by, and Moses will get to see God's backside. In Hebrew thought to see the face was to see everything of another. Moses will not see the face, so this will have to do. It is not everything, but it is something. Even for a guy like Moses, who really knows how to talk with God, he cannot see *all* of God, at least not in this life.

This reminds me of Paul the Apostle's words in 1 Corinthians 13: "For we know only in part, and we prophesy only in part; but when the complete comes, the partial will come to an end. When I was a child, I spoke like a child, I thought like a child, I reasoned like a child; when I became an adult, I put an end to childish ways. For now we see in a mirror, dimly, but then we will see *face to face*. Now I know only in part; then I will know fully, even as I have been fully known (1 Cor 13:9–12, emphasis added).

It is more than a little frustrating that we cannot "see" all of God because we have real questions, real needs, real problems. We want full assurance when we sojourn through a wilderness that everything is going to be okay. Let me see it all God. Your glory. Everything. We want to see through the cancer, the divorce, the unemployment, the doubt, and know that everything is going to work out like we want it to.

There are times I really wish I could see all of God. There are some things I would like to know. Routinely, it seems I learn of another friend diagnosed with cancer or another acquaintance succumbing to a disease or another part of the world torn asunder by war.

I would just like to see God personally about this. I have a long list of other stuff, too.

Who can blame Moses for saying, "I want full disclosure"? But even Moses, the man who listens to God, the man who argues, pleads, and negotiates with God, is still left with a partial view.

We cannot see all of the Glory of God on this side of life. We are limited. We do, however, get to stand in the cleft of the rock and see where God has been. Another way to translate "backside" in this passage is "after" or "afterward." Moses could not see God but he could see where God has been. We can see the presence and even the glory in the wake of changed and transformed lives, sometimes our own.

If I don't take the time to reflect, to look, to notice, there is a good chance I will miss where God has been. My day will be nothing more than just another place on the calendar where I can put an "x" as I get ready for what's next. Each day I need to find a cleft in the rock and sit awhile to see. There, you and I can invite others to sit with us and say, "Look, there is where God has been—glory!" We can love like Jesus and experience the glory. Soon, others are loved and brought in to experience the presence, the glory of God. I mentioned earlier that the word "glory" implies light. It was Jesus who said, "Let your light shine that they may see…and give glory" (Mt 5:16).

Years ago, one of my mentors in ministry, Bill Self, was diagnosed with Lou Gehrig's disease. He would die about a year later. Bill was the pastor of some of the largest churches in Atlanta in his day, but this disease would soon take everything away from him, including his life. When Bill was talking to his pastor about his diagnosis of ALS, he said to him: "Shaun, I want the church to know that I'm not panicked. The same God who has brought us this far, will be with me through this, too." Then after a reflective and silent pause, he added, "The One who rolls away stones is with us."

We cannot see all of God. But thank God that someone saw the stone rolled away, the tomb empty, and thank God that even at our darkest moments, if we pause in the cleft of the rock, we can see the afterglow of light burning on the horizon. Glory. Glory. Glory.

Oh, Lord, show us your ways. Show us your glory. Show up. And may the ways, love, and presence of God fill not only this place, but every life we meet.

Learning to Get Along with God

Exodus 34:1–28

Starting over. It is the mother of grown children who decides to go back to school and finish her degree. It is the college student who halfway through realizes they are in the wrong major and has to begin a new curriculum. It is the middle-aged husband, miserable in his career, who decides to resign and start a business. It is the lonely adult child who just buried their mama. Have you ever had to start something over? A marriage, a career, a recovery, a life?

This story is about Israel starting over. Stuck in the middle of nowhere, broken promises all around, including on the ground, and uncertainty about where to go from here. I love imagining God stooping down at the foot of the mountain—now the Bible does not say this is happening, but that is my image—and at the foot of the mountain God picks up those broken pieces of the tablets, the covenant, the Ten Commandments, and brushes them aside, and while dusting off his hands says, "Let's start over." We can do that; just start over. Here are a couple things that you need to know about starting over.

Sin Breaks

Sin breaks things, and not just tablets of stone. Sin breaks promises, sin breaks relationships, sin breaks people, and sin will break you, too. In our Exodus wandering, this took on a literal form with the tablets shattered to pieces. Those tablets were a reflection of the relationship broken with God. At its root, that is what sin is—a relationship broken. It is not simply about doing "bad" things or acts. It is breaking trust and without trust there is no relationship.

The consequences of sin have a systemic effect. Consider the last half of verse 7b: "Yet by no means clearing the guilty, but visiting the iniquity of the parents upon the children and the children's children, to the third and the fourth generation (Ex 34:7b).

That seems excessive, as if God holds grudges, doesn't it? There are some Jewish traditions that use this verse as instructive to parenting. When parents fail to provide for their children a good religious and moral foundation, it will impact subsequent generations. We know this to be a general truth. Systems repeat.

Sin, too, has a systemic effect. God's grace is sufficient, we read in the first half of verse 7, to the thousandth generation, but the consequences can still be felt, even for later generations. It is not an exaggeration to state, for example, that the sins of slavery and the subsequent Jim Crow laws that were in place in our country have impacted in dramatic ways the racial tensions we are experiencing 150 years later. Another example comes from the Journal of Public Health stating that many maltreated, neglected, and abused children grow and perpetuate similar cycles of abuse.[1] One more example and this one comes by way of the Pew Charitable Trust. If you are born poor, there is a 70% likelihood that you will die poor.[2] This sin of poverty repeats itself from generation to generation.

"Visiting the iniquity…to the third and fourth generation…" The sin of racism, the sin of abuse, and the sin of poverty are just three simple examples to illustrate how its consequences are felt from one generation to the next. What you do matters, and not just to you, but to those around you. God takes sin seriously, and you and I ought to, too. "God will not be mocked and grace is not cheap."[3] Sin breaks, but…

God Restores

Listen to God's words as he speaks to Moses: "The LORD passed before him, and proclaimed, 'The LORD, the LORD, a God merciful and gracious, slow to anger, and abounding in steadfast love and faithfulness, keeping steadfast love for the thousandth generation, forgiving iniquity and transgression and sin…'" (Ex 34:6–7).

In Judaism, this is referred to as the "Thirteen Attributes of God," and is recited and chanted on the High Holy Days and the Festivals. Many scholars—Jewish and Christian—see this verse as the fullest expression of the name and nature of God that we have in the Bible.

merciful
gracious
slow to anger
abounding in steadfast love
abounding in faithfulness
keeping steadfast love
forgiving iniquity

God's commitment to God's people is deep and firm. And it comes at a time when the people of God need to hear it most, because their offense is grave.

Has there ever been a time in your life when you felt as though your failure has gotten in the way of connecting with God? I have known good people going through a tough patch, like a divorce, or a personal failure, or an offense, who drop completely out of the community of church because they feel that their relationship with God is in jeopardy. And to be honest, sometimes the church can be too quick to help them out the door.

No, the people have not been good and God has not been pleased, yet God discloses to Moses that all is not hopeless. God is bigger than their sins, their shortcomings, their failures in the faith. In God's imagination, according to scripture, God's will for creation is restoration. In the final pages of the last book of the Bible, we read a voice of revelation saying, "See, I am making all things new" (Rev 21:5).

Notice what we read next: "And Moses quickly bowed his head toward the earth, and worshiped" (Ex 34:8).

If you are struggling with your worship—and all of us will from time to time struggle with our worship—it is usually not a matter of all the superficial things we think it to be about: music selection, quality of sermons, friendliness of the congregation. Of course all of those things are important, but not most important. No, if you are struggling with your worship, it probably goes back to one of the two areas I have mentioned from this story: it is a matter of sin (broken relationship) or a matter of restoration, or both.

Sin separates us from God and from others and therefore worship will struggle. Sin reduces worship to an entertainment event that will never measure up. We are all sinners here, so on some level, our worship will always be less than whole. Sin unaddressed, denied, or otherwise ignored will be a wedge dividing us against each another and God.

Likewise, restoration is foundational to worship. Restoration is being reconciled with one another. It is restoring and renewing relationships with friends, family, strangers, and of course God. Restored is the alcoholic who walks away from the bottle. Restored is the victim of abuse who decided they will no longer be defined by their past. Restored is the one who was denied justice but now has been set free. Every Sunday, we come dragging our chains that have weighed us down and, every Sunday, we need to remind each other that God wants to do something about it.

For Israel and the dust of its idolatry and the fragments of their covenant littered at the foot of the mountain, God wants to revisit creation and make something new again. Moses responds by worship: "And Moses quickly bowed his head toward earth, and worshiped."

If you are struggling with worship—and, like I said, we all struggle from time to time in our worship—before you look for something different, or new, or better, I invite you to ask two foundational questions:

1. Is it because of sin (mine or the sin of others)?
2. Is it a matter of restoration?

Yes, I realize those are tough questions. Some may even say it sounds too judgmental. I am not asking you to judge others. I am asking you to reflect on just how serious God takes matters of sin and restoration in your life.

Moses then prays a prayer we need to hear so many centuries later: "If now I have found favor in your sight, O Lord, I pray, let the Lord go with us. Although this is a stiff-necked people, pardon our iniquity and our sin, and take us for your inheritance" (Ex 34:9). Moses' prayer is our prayer: God, go with us, forgive us, and do not forget us.

That is why authentic worship necessitates a response. We leave with the prayer of Moses in some form or another: God, you know when I leave here I am still facing problems with my parents. Lord, you know I am struggling with my job. God, you know the secret thoughts of my heart, my struggles, and my temptations. "Lord, go with us…pardon our iniquity…take us for your inheritance."

Hear how God responds to Moses: "I hereby make a covenant." (There is that word again, covenant. It is mentioned over three hundred times in the scriptures.) "Before all your people I will perform marvels, such as have not been performed in all the earth or in any nation; and all the people among whom you live shall see the work of the LORD; for it is an awesome thing that I will do with you…" (Ex 34:10).

For all of us wanting to start over, let these ancient words give you a new life. You can start over, right now. Sin most certainly destroys and its impact can go on for generations. But more important than sin, God wants to make all things new, and that includes you. And me, too.

[1] Julie Taylor, Caroline Bradbury-Jones, Anne Lazenbatt, Francesca Soliman, "Child maltreatment: pathway to chronic and long-term conditions?" *Journal of Public Health*, Volume 38, Issue 3, 17 September 2016, Pages 426–431, https://doi.org/10.1093/pubmed/fdv117.

[2] Robert Oak, "You're Born Into It America," *The Economic Populist*, January 11, 2012, http://www.economicpopulist.org/content/youre-born-it-america.

[3] Walter Brueggemann, *New Interpreters Bible Commentary, Volume 1* (Nashville TN: 1994), 947.

Face Up and Look Out

Exodus 34:29–35

In the previous sermon, we heard of God's commitment to pick up the pieces and start over with Israel. The first time Moses descended the Mountain of God with two tablets in his hand he was shocked to find Israel in disarray worshipping a homemade god. This time it is the Israelites who are unsettled as they see Moses transformed, changed, and glowing.

We have heard this story before, well, one like it. In the New Testament, it is Jesus who climbs a mountain, has a moment with God, and is transfigured by the experience. For Jesus, it was probably a different mountain, and, unlike Moses, Jesus has a few more people on the mountain with him. Like Moses, Jesus' countenance changes.

For forty days and nights, Moses (and remember he has done this before) has listened, spoken, and encountered God. Now he descends the mountain transfigured by God and shining. That word, "shining," is an unusual word in the Bible. It is only used here, but elsewhere is translated as horn, like that on an animal. Michelangelo carved a statue of Moses with horns coming out of us head. Modern translations, however, use the word "shine."

The sight was unsettling. We read that Aaron and the leaders and the Israelites were afraid to come near him. Moses has "gotten religious" and that is a bit frightening. Of course, this is not about getting religious. It is about a holy encounter that changes the way Moses sees things and the way others see Moses.

We all hunger for that kind of transformation with God, don't we? Theologian Rudolf Otto says that we are both drawn to God and yet terrified of holy encounters.[1] Deep inside, even among the most profane, is a yearning for sacred significance. We want something, someone to stir us deep down so that our face literally radiates Holy Goodness; something, someone who will leave us shining, shimmering, and beaming transcendent.

Without the glow of God, the world is flattened, dull, and exists only for what we can self-indulgently get out of it. Without the glory of God filling us and inspiring us, dangerous things happen from death camps about the world to riotous violence in our own land.

And so we hunger throughout our lives to enter into something deeper, something of significance, something eternal—a vision for life. This story challenges us to...

See the world as God sees.

People who have been transformed and encounter God see the world differently; see the neighbor differently; see the enemy differently. Faces glow and radiate something deeper inside; something beyond category. Moses left that mountain no longer with a vision of what *he* needed to do, or what *he* wanted from Israel or what *he* was expecting when they cross the Jordan to enter the Promised Land. Moses left the mountain seeing, at least in part, as God sees.

Seeing the world as God sees is not about being a pessimist or optimist or realist or idealist. It is about a transformation of vision. How do you see the world? Is the glass half full, half empty, drained to the dregs, or flowing over the rim? How do you see the world and those around you?

What if we saw the world through God's eyes? How would it look? How would we look? More to the point, what does God see?

1. Brokenness and sin. Some scholars argue that the first 11 chapters of Genesis are an accounting of the limping, brokenness of humankind. I suspect we see that, too. We see how badly people have failed. Jesus challenged, "Let the one who is without sin cast the first stone," and we discover that there are no stones available. Every Sunday that someone joins the church, we are welcoming another sinner into the congregation. Next thing you know this place will be full of sinners! At least that is what I think God sees. Do you see what God sees?

2. Struggles and weakness. Life is hard. Our bodies fail us, our minds deceive us, others disappoint us. God sees all this, as well as the pain and suffering around the world. Do you see what God sees?

3. Beauty. When God created the world, God called it good. Now just because we are outside of Eden does not take away the "original blessing" as Matthew Fox calls it. The character Shug, in the novel *The Color Purple*, said it well: "I think it makes God angry if you walk by the color purple in a field somewhere and don't notice it."[2] Do you see what God sees?

4. Possibility and potential. Creation was not a static event but an unfolding journey. When we are baptized, we are told to walk in "newness of

life" and it was Jesus who said he had come to give us life and "to have it abundantly." Do you see what God sees?

God sees the brokenness and sin; God sees the struggles and weaknesses; God sees the beauty and potential. God sees all of this and more. Maybe that is why God chose to look upon Moses and set his face aglow. Moses was coming down the mountain to share with Israel what we call The Ten Commandments, but rather than law and doctrine, you first need to have an encounter, a relationship. Believing is fine, it is essential, but without transformation, it just becomes another policy or statement.

Jesus made connections and transformed relationships that we may see as God sees. In John 1:14 we read, "We have seen his glory, the glory as of a father's only son, full of grace and truth." To see the world as God sees is an invitation to change your vision.

Are you willing to do that? When you spend time with God and enter into holy places, you risk having your vision changed to see as God sees, which means we are going to judge less and love more. It means we are going to seek the welfare of others and not just think about our own needs. It means we are going to give to the underserved, believing God can change hearts and minds.

When you see the world as God sees, you... respond as God responds.

That is what happens with vision, right? The eye takes in data, which is delivered to the brain, and the brain interprets that data and we respond accordingly. When you change your vision, you change how you act.

When Moses descended the mountain, he glowed with presence to lead Israel into promise. Up until this point, Moses was leading mostly according to his own terms. As Israel complained, he complained. When Israel broke faith, Moses broke tablets. Now all of this is changing like the skin on his body. Spending time with God is not just about more Bible study, more sermons, more prayer, or more lessons. It is about seeing as God sees and therefore *responding* in the world accordingly.

When you see as God sees, you begin to see how God is present even in the most inglorious of situations. With God's glory, we have a vision that changes things. The worst of humanity is not the final word or act or decisive narrative of creation. God has something far better to show us.

For all this to unfold in your life, you have to climb the mountain and spend time with God—wrestling, praying, arguing, hoping, longing, searching—but you need to come down that mountain prepared to do something.

When you see as God sees and respond as God responds... others see God in you.

They see a reflection of the glory, the hope, the salvation. No, they do not see everything of God just like no other person can see everything of you. To be transfigured is to change how you see and therefore to be changed in how you are seen by others.

This takes us back to my remarks earlier: deep down we all want something that is beyond category; beyond the old and dull and banal. We want a holy vitality, a vigor in life, and a vision for the horizon. That is why worship is so critical to the church. It is not about favorite hymns or praise songs. Goodness knows, it is not about being entertained. We may all articulate it differently, but I believe, whether we know it or not, we want a fiery transformation. We want to walk away glowing, seeing differently, and therefore being seen differently.

Sometimes this happens in a gallery or museum where a painting overwhelms you. I remember so well standing with my wife in a small corner of Santa Maria del Popolo, in Rome, Italy. To our left was a painting by Caravaggio, depicting the calling of St. Paul and to the right he had painted the crucifixion of St. Peter. I can't describe it but there was something about the juxtaposition of the paintings of these two men dying to something that left me a bit lightheaded. Sometimes transformation happens after a concert or solo where the music stirs your heart and you did not expect it but you start crying.

Perhaps it is too much to ask this of worship every Sunday. Transformation may only come once in a lifetime for some of us. Yet we need to climb this mountain every Sunday to seek the face of God in our music, in our prayers, in our silence, and in our proclamation.

Every Sunday, I close worship with the words from Numbers Chapter 6: "May the Lord make his face shine upon you" (Num. 6:25). That is the blessing I want. That is the blessing I need. That is how I want to leave church—glowing, radiant, with a new vision, and a new life. Not because I heard a great anthem, or that the sermon really spoke to me. I want, I need to have an encounter, not with a static word or command, something written on stone, but with the Living Lord who wants to change how I see and change how I live and transform how I am seen, for God's good glory.

Melissa Bane Sevier states: "When you've spent time with God, you reflect God's joy, God's pain, the glow of the search for an answer or the ability to live with the questions, the clarity of God's presence or the luminous desire for that presence. And, whether you know it or not, someone else will notice."[3] Paul the Apostle writes, "And all of us, with unveiled faces, seeing the glory of the Lord as though reflected in a mirror, are being transformed into the same image from one degree of glory to another; for this comes from the Lord, the Spirit" (2 Cor 3:18).

Indeed, is this not the purpose of the church? To reflect the Glory of God; to let our light shine, as Jesus said in Matthew 5:16, "…so that they may see your good works and give glory to your Father in heaven."

Like Moses, the Glory of God will change you.

Like Jesus, the Glory of God will change the world.

The Glory of God changes you from the inside out. You see differently. You act differently. You are different. Glorious is Thy name!

---

[1] *The Idea of the Holy*, trans JW Harvey, (New York: OUP, 1923; 2nd edition, 1950; reprint, New York, 1970).

[2] Alice Walker, *The Color Purple*, 10th Anniversary ed. (New York: Harcourt Brace Jovanovich, 1992) 191.

[3] Melissa Ban Sevier, "Shiny Faces," *Contemplative Viewfinder* (blog), February 8, 2010, https://melissabanesevier.wordpress.com/2010/02/08/shiny-faces/.

Missio Dei:
A People at Work
Exodus 35:1–40:38

Saying Yes

Exodus 35:1–39:43

The *Missio Dei*—the mission of God—sounds big, doesn't it? Almost too big. It is difficult enough to comprehend one's own personal mission. During spring, we are immersed with images of graduations, large and small: from high school, from technical colleges, and from universities. Some of our friends and family graduate magna cum laude and others graduate "Thank You, Lawdy." Either way, now the life's mission begins! Do you have what it takes?

Israel has made a jagged journey through the wilderness and both God and the people have made a commitment to start over on the *Missio Dei*. God has a big enterprise for Israel to join in and God has a big enterprise for you and me, too. Of course, you have to say yes in order to be part of a mission that is bigger than you, bigger than any one of us.

When God invited Israel to start over, Israel had the opportunity to say "yes…I am with you and ready to offer what I have." Part of this starting over involved a recommitment to the constructing of the Tabernacle, the Tent of Meeting. This structure represented to Israel that God was with them wherever they go.

I regret that too often this story is used to promote church construction or debt retirement or otherwise raise money. This is not concerned with one's financial stewardship. This is about stewardship of life. Your life in God's mission. And as they go, everyone had something to offer.

Exodus 35:21 says, "And they came, everyone whose heart was stirred, and everyone whose spirit was willing…" Everyone had something to offer. We read in Chapters 35 through 39 that artisans, metallurgists, carpenters, bankers, perfumers, and wood carvers are used in this recommitment. Musicians are not mentioned here but we know the great contribution they make throughout the Bible.

I am getting ahead of myself. The point is, as Israel starts over with its commitment to God, the only thing really needed was a *willing spirit*.

We know that there are times we need to start over. Starting over is to: Renew a friendship that has been neglected over the passage of time because of a slight or an offense. Rededicate a commitment made long ago that has now lost focus and enthusiasm. Or just simply begin again. It is one thing to say I want to start over, but it is another thing to know how to start over.

It begins with a willing spirit. Just saying yes is the first step to preparing a place for God in your life. Israel needed that Tabernacle as a way to worship along the way and be reminded that God goes with them in and through the desert. They said yes to God and it made a difference of abundance.

At some point in the life of every soul, we are confronted with questions that bear eternal significance. It is a yes/no kind of question. In our lifetime, we will be asked whether to say yes to God or no to God.

Israel's story is one of a people who said yes to God. Well, sort of. They said yes, and complained that they were going to starve to death out in the wilderness. They said yes, and then grumbled that they were tired of eating manna every day. They said yes, and then they erected a golden calf. They said yes, and then when they came to the borders of the Promised Land they feared to enter in. But they did say yes. Now they come to a place in their journey to establish themselves; to finally make a place for God, and it started with a willing spirit. They said yes.

You are here because, on some level, you have said yes to God. It may be an uncertain and tepid yes, but it is a yes all the same. Like Thomas, it may be a doubting skeptical yes. But nonetheless, here we are. God has spoken and we have responded, "Well okay. Yes."

When I was junior in college, preparing for seminary, a small country church in the foothills of northwest Georgia invited me to preach for a few Sundays in the fall. After a month or so of Sunday services, the deacons of the church, four or five as I recall, invited me to dinner. It was there, I was surprised to learn, that they asked me to serve as their pastor. It seemed ridiculous to me at the time that they should ask a 21-year-old to be their pastor, still I said yes anyway. I said yes to a deacon body and a congregation, even though I had no idea what I was getting into. I did not know, really, what I was doing. The real work was ahead of me…and I still do not know about the implications of my yes. We can make similar claims in our marriage proposals and planning a family.

What we can do with our "yes" is bring to God *everything*. "The people are bringing much more than enough for doing the work that the LORD has commanded us to do" (Ex 36:5). What will you and I do because we have said yes to God? How will you and I make a difference in this world? Instead of talking about the problems, how can we actively participate in solutions? Saying "yes" is giving back to God what is God's already—our very life. *"...the one who sows sparingly will also reap sparingly, and the one who sows bountifully will also reap bountifully"* (2 Cor 9:6).

When we say yes, we give back to God through our:

Vocation

A third of our life will be spent sleeping, a third of our life will be spent doing a variety of things, and about a third of our adult years will be spent working a job, career, or something that interacts with others. Our vocation cannot be separated from the claims of God.

Community

We seem to confuse, however, politicking with community involvement. God has called us into community, to be engaged with others.

Family

Marriages ought to be different. The way we treat our parents ought to be different. The way we raise our kids ought to be different. Too often I hear of children who seem to dictate to parents what part their faith plays in their life, instead of parents lovingly modeling faith.

Church

The strength of a church is not in its pastor—it is in the people. I invite you to find your place here. We read in the previous chapter that Moses sought out "…all who were skillful…" (Ex 35:10). Say yes to the future of your church, not as a bystander, but a participant. Your life too deserves a big and audacious "Yes."

What God needs—if I may be so presumptuous to say—is our yes. But just because of our yes, we will still not be perfect. We will not get it right all the time. We will blow it and miss the mark. But still, because of our yes, God can do and does great things.

All we need to bring is ourselves. It is more than enough.

Exodus 36:6—"the people were restrained from bringing…"

Finishing What You Start

Exodus 40:1–33

One day I was at Costco and ran into a former neighbor. As we were catching up on each other's lives, he commented that he was keeping up with me through the church's television broadcast where I was serving as pastor. I asked him about his church home. He shared with me where he was a church member, but that he was a little displeased because of the cost of the church's recent building project. This led into a larger conversation of the cost of church buildings. All over the world there are structures built at great cost presumably out of devotion and veneration to God.

One would think from reading Exodus that the entire purpose and enterprise of the exodus of Israel from Egypt was not the Promised Land, but a building project—specifically the completion of the Tabernacle, or the Tent of Meeting as it is also called. The completion of this project comes just two weeks shy of the first anniversary of the exodus from Egypt. At this point in the journey there really has not been much wandering—just escaping and getting ready to march onward towards God's distant promise. We really have to wait until the book of Numbers before reading about their move and that will not end until 39 years later in the book of Joshua. Before they can load the biblical station wagon and go any further, this Tabernacle building project needs to be completed.

The Tabernacle is more than just a meeting place; more than just a mobile shrine. It is a shadow of what heaven is to be like. We have our own versions: a delicately planted corner in the backyard; a private study adorned with tokens of the past; or a sanctuary where you gather Sunday after Sunday to worship.

I will spare you the details, which you can read for yourself, but someone estimated that the market value of the Tabernacle—remember this is a tent!—is approximately $57 million.[1] Like a Fabergé egg, it is not that large but the details are nearly priceless.

Why is it so important, this Tabernacle? We know more about the construction of the Tabernacle in the wilderness than we do the mighty Temple that once stood in Jerusalem. Half of Exodus is dedicated to the Tabernacle's construction. We remember baby Moses floating down the Nile and God speaking from a burning bush. The plagues are interesting, too (unless you are a victim), and the parting of the Red Sea is unforgettable. All of those stories are told in just a few verses within a few chapters. But the Tabernacle makes up half of the book. And let's be honest, it is not that interesting.

The Tabernacle was for Israel the cosmos in miniature. It is creation as God would have it to be; heaven on earth. "They offer worship in a sanctuary that is a sketch and shadow of the heavenly one…" (Heb. 8:5). Through the symbolism of the Tabernacle, God is dwelling with the very people who are to be a blessing to the world.

God knows the world needs, hungers, and thirsts for a holy blessing. These are god-forsaken times, but then again times are always feeling god-forsaken. War, violence, exploitation, hatred, greed, bigotry are not modern inventions. We have just gotten more sophisticated about our god-forsaken ways.

The world needs the blessing that God still wants to pitch a tent with us and has not given up and gone back to heaven. Israel was to be that blessing to the nations and the Tabernacle was that vessel to symbolize God is with us. God will not be left on Mt. Sinai or in Heaven, but will be with the people in the wandering, in the wilderness, in the Promised Land, and throughout time.

The Tabernacle included rituals and rites to deal with bridging the chasm between Holy God and fallen creation. Sin is the tear in creation, mangling all relationships on heaven *and* earth. It has environmental consequences, and so we scoff at holes in the ozone layer and disappearing forests, even though God gave us the earth and told us to take care of it. It has familial consequences, and so homes are in disarray, marriages fail, and children are exploited, even though God told us to honor, love, care, and sacrifice for each other. Of course, sin ultimately has consequences in our relationship with God. What we disrupt on earth, disrupts heaven, and deep is the chasm.

Moses had to finish this project because Israel needed to know God wants to bridge the gap, and not just with Israel, but with all the world. In the very beginning of time, we read stories of God wanting to be with the people. Eden was the garden where God walked and talked with creation. Sin destroyed the intent of creation and we have been reeling ever since.

Why do we Christians, living in the 21st century, need to understand the Tabernacle of an ancient time, with all its superstitious beliefs? Some will argue that we have the clearest example of who Jesus Christ is, not in the Gospels, but in the imagery of the Tabernacle. Here are three reasons why:

1. Christ is the fulfillment of God with us.

The Gospel of John begins with this affirmation. We read in John 1.14, "And the Word became flesh and lived among us…" In the original Greek, it literally reads he "pitched his tent" among us.

A few years ago, I was backpacking with a friend and, as we were ambling along the trail, it was apparent that a storm was brewing. We decided it would be best to change our destination for the night from an exposed area along creek bottoms that would no doubt flood, to an elevated side of a mountain. During the night we were joined by other backpackers. By morning there were nearly a dozen other hikers who had pitched their tents along with ours. It was an oddly comforting sight to know that we were not alone and that we were in this together.

Christ provides what no structure on earth can ever do: the presence of God here on this earth and, through the Holy Spirit, God's presence continues to abide.

As such the Tabernacle became a literal picture of God in the world but not of the world. The tabernacle is the dwelling place of God and as such represents God dwelling with the people.

2. Christ is the complete sacrifice.

The Tabernacle provided a way or a mechanism for the ritual cleansing of sin. This included sacrifices made throughout the year. In Leviticus, we read of five sacrifices that are to be made each year, four of which involved the blood of animals as substitute for the Israelites own blood.

This is not a matter of God needing a blood offering. The ancient Israelites nevertheless understood that their sin was deadly and in order to be clean before God, sacrifices had to be made. Unlike some of the surrounding cultures, Israel did not practice human sacrifice, therefore animals were substituted. Only the high priest can approach God in the Holy of Holies in the center of the sanctuary. Its structure has many barriers between the sinful people and the seat of God that is reflected in its structure.

In the Christian tradition Jesus ended all of that by becoming the complete offering. In Hebrews, we read: "Unlike the other high priests, he has no need to offer sacrifices day after day, first for his own sins, and then for those of the people; this he did once for all when he offered himself" (Heb. 7:27).

3. Christ takes us into the Being of God (Holy of Holies).

The Gospel of Matthew records that at the point of Jesus' death on the cross the curtain of the Temple—that which separates the Holy of Holies—was torn from top to bottom. Symbolically, Jesus bridged heaven and earth. "But when Christ came as a high priest of the good things that have come, then through the greater and perfect tent (not made with hands, that is, not of this creation), he entered once for all into the Holy Place, not with the blood of goats and calves, but with his own blood, thus obtaining eternal redemption" (Heb. 9:11-12).

In the last chapter of this mighty book, we read the words from verse 33: "So Moses finished the work" (Ex 40:33). This in itself is an interesting phrase. It is the same one we find in the Creation story in Genesis 2: "And on the seventh day God finished the work…"

Jesus began a good work in this world and in the resurrection finished what God started. Except it is not quite finished, is it? We too began a walk with God. Like Israel, we have gotten off the trail from time to time. Like Israel, we grumble, complain, question, and even doubt. Sometimes we quit. That is why we need to finish what we started. We still need tabernacles.

Earlier, I shared a brief story about backpacking. Nowadays it is not uncommon to see backpackers forgo tents for lighter gear such as a hammock or just sleeping on the ground with a simple tarp. I still like a tent. On the trail it can feel a bit like home. It is just a shadow, of course, but it is something.

I think that one of the essential functions for a church is to "tabernacle" alongside others to be God's presence, God's grace, and God's mercy along life's journey. We can pitch our tent with others who are stumbling through the wilderness trying to make their way home. We pitch our tent to the one wandering; to the one grieving; to the hungry and helpless. We pitch our tent and remember that we can be that blessing to the other.

God knows the world needs it, so what is holding you, us, back? It is time to move out and march on. The wilderness awaits.

"For Christ did not enter a sanctuary made by human hands, a mere copy of the true one, but he entered into heaven itself, now to appear in the presence of God on our behalf" (Heb. 9:24),

[1] Danny Ferguson, "What would the it cost to build the Tabernacle described in Exodus?" *Proyouthworker*, January 5, 2011, http://www.proyouthworker.com/2011/01/what-would-it-cost-to-build-tabernacle.html.

To God Be the Glory

Exodus 40:34–38

After 40 chapters, 37 sermons, multiple cross-references from other parts of the Bible, we now come to the completion of the Book of Exodus. There is one word I think best describes the second book of the Torah and that is: Epic!

If you are a movie buff, the *Star Wars* trilogy of the 1970s and '80s is an epic story of light, darkness, and mission in a galaxy far, far away. If you are into fantasy novels, then *Lord of the Rings* is an epic story of good, evil, and redemption of the land. If you are into adventure, the summiting of Mount Everest by Edmund Hillary and Tenzing Norgay is an epic feat of overcoming the largest obstacle on the planet.

Exodus is epic. It is easy to think that Exodus is about Moses, but it is not. Moses will never even make it in the Promised Land, but dies on a different mountain, Mt. Nebo, and is buried in an unmarked grave in the valley. This is not a story about Moses or Aaron or Joshua or Miriam or Pharaoh or any other person. This is a story about God and in particular the *Missio Dei*, the mission of God.

Like I said, it is epic. The story of Exodus is part of the larger gospel of *Missio Dei*. Israel's experience is part of the greater story of God at work since the foundation of creation, and if that is not epic then I do not know what is.

In the book of Exodus, we read of the LORD God working through the particular people called Israel to bring about liberation and deliverance and, along the way, we read of their wanderings, apostasy, grumblings, and restoration. This is a story about a particular people in a particular time. And yet it is also a story for all people of all times. Exodus is the church's story. It is your story and it is my story.

God is still at work in this world, from one generation to the next, in a mission of liberation, healing, and redemption. We are invited to join with God in that holy enterprise of setting people free. In joining God we also recognize our own need for healing and redemption. Walter Brueggemann writes of the Exodus story, "…it provides for us the essential characters and the recurring plot that is always being performed and re-performed in the world."[1]

In Exodus, we witness a "contextualization" of the good news of God speaking to weakness and power, to enslavement and liberation, to deliverance and inheritance. As witnesses, we listen for our call of God, see the brokenness of our world, and reimagine what could be. This work inevitably involves its own kind of wilderness wandering along with failures, sin, and broken faith. Yet YHWH invites us back into covenant and restoration as we move forward into a world waiting to be set free.

So where have we been in the last 40 chapters and what have seen? The story begins in Chapter 1 with forgetting. The Pharaoh forgets where all these Hebrew slaves came from and forgets who their God is. Meanwhile, the Hebrews feel as though God has forgotten about them—they are slaves and Pharaoh wants to work them to death and wipe them out in the process. Baby boys are tossed in the Nile to die because Pharaoh said there were too many of them, but in Chapter 2, we read that one little boy survives: Moses, whose name means to "draw out." Moses grows up and is called out by God from a burning bush to draw the people out of Egypt and into a land promised. The delivered becomes the deliverer. Pharaoh says no to "let my people go" and ten plagues later he says, "Well, maybe." But Pharaoh has a hard heart and a head to match and by Chapter 14 chases these fleeing Israelites all the way to the Red Sea, which Moses parts for his people and then collapses on Pharaoh and all his chariots.

Out of this dislocated world, God, who is now personally known as YHWH, wants Moses and the Israelites to reimagine the world as it could be; as it should be; as God intended it to be. The Passover observance, that was instituted before leaving Egypt, is not just remembering the Angel of Death passing over the Israelites at the expense of the Egyptians. Passover was and is a new start for all who choose to believe in God's mission for life. Yet for the remainder of Exodus, many of these newly emancipated Hebrews believe more in their insecurity and hunger and so remain enslaved by their fear and appetites. Still, God provides and so by Chapter 16 we read of water in the desert and bread from the sky.

Though we tend to think of Moses as a hero-warrior, the story also tells of his all too human character, complete with flaws and weaknesses. He has a father-in-law to remind him that he cannot do this on his own. He has friends to stand beside him and prop him up in battle. Still Moses is God's man for the season and, in Chapters 20 through 25, God calls him up to the Mountain of God, Mount Sinai, and gives him the Ten Commandments, Ten

Words as the Jews call them, that read as a map to guide the Israelites on how to live with God by living with one another.

We read of Israel continuing to falter in their newfound freedom. In Chapter 32, the golden calf is an ugly example and it looks like God might just stay on the mountain and let Israel march on without God. In the end, Moses does not give up and neither does God. Out of the broken covenant and broken relationship they start over and move on to finish the construction project of the Tabernacle. From Chapter 35 to the end of the book, we read how this structure is to remind Israel that God is serious about being present in their lives, serious about the people being clean and consecrated, and serious about dwelling with them in the wilderness and beyond. The Tabernacle is reinterpreted in early Christian history as the archetype of Christ. Jesus finishes what the tabernacle started.

Even though there is much motion in Exodus, these ancient Hebrews have not gone far. From the Red Sea to the end of this book, only a year has passed and they have traveled just 44 of those days. One hundred and sixty-one miles later, they are parked at the foot of the Mountain of God and have gone no further in the wilderness.

We come to the end of this epic story only to realize the real journey is just beginning. In some ways, Exodus ends much like the ending of the final movie of the trilogy *Lord of the Rings*, where the character Frodo tells his friends he will not be able to inherit the land with them. In his final line, Frodo says: "Your part in the story will go on."[2]

Israel is about to pull up the tent pegs and plunge deep in the wilderness where they will wander for the next 39 years. The screen credits are about to roll and the closing scene is upon us. What we read in these final verses is that the glory of God covers the tabernacle, the tent of meeting, in the form of a cloud by day and fire by night. If God's glory remained, the people would stay put. If the glory moved on, so would the people. The last verse of the last chapter of this epic book reads: "For the cloud of the LORD was on the tabernacle by day, and fire was in the cloud by night, before the eyes of all the house of Israel at each stage of their journey (Ex 40:38).

The book that begins in the darkness of their misery ends with the Light of God's glory. From now on, Israel dare not go where the Glory of God does not lead.

As I said, Exodus is not just the story of ancient Israel. It is our story, too. It is the church's story, your story, and my story. We, too, know about darkness and hopelessness where our experiences feel God-forsaken. We have spiritual high points like Mount Sinai and we have low moments complaining in the desert. We know what it is like to feel the power of God on our side with plagues upon our enemies, and we have tasted the failure of our apostasy with our own golden calves.

God's commitment is to move you, to move us, to move creation from the chaos and darkness into the light of promise. As Exodus closes, we have these poignant reminders for our own trajectory of life. Exodus tells us that this life is never about any one of us, but all of us. And, for all of us, Exodus is the epic narrative of God's mission to the world and our purpose is to be part in it.

You cannot lead a life of purpose without God filling you and leading you.

You cannot live a life that matters without God filling you and leading you.

We cannot partner with the Mission of God without God filling us and leading us.

Like Israel, we dare not go where the Glory of God does not lead.

To matter in life, God needs to matter in your life. God's Glory is not an add-on to your plans; not a sub-set to your life's mission; and certainly not an afterthought to your priorities. Remember that the indwelling of the Holy Spirit is the peculiar presence of God's Glory that liberates, enlivens, and lights up our movement to the promise.

If we follow the Glory of God, it takes us into the mission of God. Exodus is that epic story that is echoed in the final words of Jesus before his ascension into heaven: "Go therefore and make disciples of all nations, baptizing them in the name of the Father and of the Son and of the Holy Spirit, and teaching them to obey everything that I have commanded you. And remember, I am with you always, to the end of the age" (Mt 28:19–20).

The complete Tabernacle; the fullness of God's Glory. What are you waiting for? You have a life to live and if you follow the Glory of God it will be an epic one.

---

[1] Walter Brueggemann, *Truth Speaks to Power* (Louisville: Westminster John Knox, 2013), 16.

[2] *The Lord of the Rings: The Return of the King*, directed by Peter Jackson, based on a novel written by J.R.R. Tolkien, featuring Elijah Wood, Ian McKellen, Liv Tyler, Viggo Mortensen, Sean Astin, Cate Blanchett, John Rhys-Davies, Christopher Lee, Billy Boyd, Dominic Monaghan, Orlando Bloom, Hugo Weaving, Andy Serkis and Sean Bean, (Los Angeles, California: New Line Cinema, 2003), DVD.

Dr. C. Gregory DeLoach became interim dean of the James and Carolyn McAfee School of Theology at Mercer University on August 1, 2018. He also serves as director of development for McAfee and the College of Professional Advancement at Mercer University.

A native of Eatonton, Dr. DeLoach has pastored congregations throughout Georgia for nearly three decades, including in Mansfield, Chickamauga, Marietta, and Augusta. Following 10 years as senior pastor of First Baptist Augusta, he became executive director of Developmental Disabilities Ministries, an Atlanta-based nonprofit, charitable corporation serving adults with developmental disabilities and their families through operation of 19 homes across Georgia. In February 2017, he joined the development staff at Mercer, having previously served on the University's Board of Trustees.

Dr. DeLoach earned his Bachelor of Science from Shorter College, Master of Divinity from Southern Baptist Theological Seminary and Doctor of Ministry from Columbia Theological Seminary. He and his wife, Amy, have two adult sons, Clark and Aaron.

www.ingramcontent.com/pod-product-compliance
Lightning Source LLC
Chambersburg PA
CBHW070844160426
43192CB00012B/2300